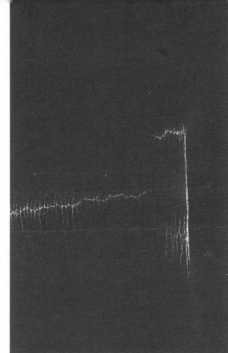

Madhur Jaffrey's
CURRY NATION

EBURY
PRESS

This book is dedicated to Britain,
the Curry Nation that welcomed me all those many years ago

Madhur Jaffrey's
CURRY NATION
Britain's 100 Favourite Recipes

EBURY
PRESS

10 9 8 7 6 5 4 3 2 1

Published in 2012 by Ebury Press,
an imprint of Ebury Publishing
A Random House Group Company
Text © Madhur Jaffrey 2012
Photography © Ebury Press 2012

Madhur Jaffrey's Curry Nation is a Cactus Production
for Good Food Channel

The Random House Group Limited Reg. No. 954009
Addresses for companies within the Random House Group
can be found at www.randomhouse.co.uk
A CIP catalogue record for this book is available from the
British Library

The Random House Group Limited supports
The Forest Stewardship Council (FSC®), the
leading international forest certification organisation.
Our books carrying the FSC label are printed on FSC®
certified paper. FSC is the only forest certification scheme
endorsed by the leading environmental organisations,
including Greenpeace. Our paper procurement policy can
be found at www.randomhouse.co.uk/environment

MIX
Paper from
responsible sources
FSC® C016897

To buy books by your favourite authors and register
for offers visit www.randomhouse.co.uk

Recipe development by Nikita Gulhane

Project editor: Lucy Bannell
Design: Pene Parker
Photography: Jean Cazals
Food styling: Katie Giovanni
Props styling: Cynthia Inions

Printed and bound by Butler Tanner and Dennis Ltd, Frome
ISBN 9780091949938

Contents

Introduction   6

Appetisers, snacks and soups   12

Lamb, pork and beef   34

Eggs and chicken   64

Fish and seafood   84

Vegetables   100

Dals   124

Rice, breads and pancakes   140

Salads, pickles, chutneys
    and relishes   172

Drinks and sweets   194

Spice mixes   212

Seasonings, techniques and
    kitchen equipment   218

Index   220

Introduction

If Britain once colonised India, India has now returned the favour by watching spellbound as its food completely colonised Britain.

The Hindostanee Coffee House was the first Indian restaurant ever to open its doors to the British public in the early nineteenth century. Its owner, Dean Mahomed, had served under a British officer in India and followed him to Britain. The restaurant was situated on George Street, near London's trendy Portman Square, and offered diners the comforts of the hubble bubble pipe as well as 'Indian dishes, in the highest perfection, and allowed by the greatest epicures to be unequalled to any curries ever made in England'. It filed for bankruptcy within two short years, as it could not entice enough customers.

Shift the scene to 2012. Today there are about 10,000 Indian restaurants, employing 80,000 staff, making the industry worth £3 billion according to one source, and accounting for two-thirds of all those who dine out. 'Going for an Indian' has become a commonplace way to spend the evening. Indian food in supermarkets alone is worth well over £600 million. This includes ready-meals and spicy sandwiches. Each Thursday night, every branch of the popular Wetherspoons pub chain turns into a Curry Club, offering 'a curry and a pint' for a reasonable price. It sells more than 70,000 curry meals every Thursday, or 3.6 million annually.

How times have changed. The sad Hindostanee Coffee House, Britain's first Indian restaurant, has now been recognised, some 200 years later, with the Mayor of Westminster unveiling a green plaque at the site. What is more, the country's former favourite dish, fish and chips, has been replaced by chicken tikka masala, leading the former Foreign Secretary Robin Cook, in a speech celebrating Britishness, to declare, 'Chicken tikka masala is now a true British national dish, not only because it is the most popular, but because it is a perfect illustration of the way Britain absorbs and adapts external influences. Chicken tikka is an Indian dish. The masala sauce was added to satisfy the desire of the British people to have their meat served in gravy.' Wetherspoons sells 15,000 servings of it every single week, apart from all the other curries. Marks & Spencer sells 18 tonnes of it a week. If all the chicken tikka masala served in Britain in one year was piled up, it would form a tower 2,270 times taller than the Millennium Dome.

Very recently, I was sitting in front of a mirror in Leicester being made up for a film. The make-up artist, Meinir Jones-Lewis, told me a story in her lilting Welsh accent. A friend, a Welsh actor, was visiting her in London. He wanted to go to a proper

Indian restaurant, which would surely be superior to anything in Cardiff. Once there, he called the waiter and ordered 'a chicken vindaloo, 'alf and 'alf.' The waiter looked puzzled. The actor repeated his request, slowly, more clearly and more loudly. The waiter still did not understand. The actor then turned to the seemingly dim-witted waiter and yelled, 'Chicken vindaloo with 'alf rice and 'alf chips!' That is how some people eat it in Wales.

Britain has, indeed, adapted Indian 'curry' to the way it wants it and this varies in different parts of the country. The meaning of the word itself has changed and evolved, in keeping both with the demands of the British people and with the changing, complex relationship between Britain and India.

This relationship started in 1600 with the formation of the East India Company. By the start of the eighteenth century, trade with India was flourishing. As it expanded and East Indiamen spread out into the Indian heartland looking for spices, saltpetre (for gunpowder), salt and indigo, they had to eat, and the only fresh food to be had was Indian. Many took to it with a passion and, in letters home, often included recipes to set out a fuller picture of their exotic lives. Those who had profited mightily from their trading returned home early with their newly acquired wealth and, sometimes, Indian servants in tow and, now designated 'nabobs', settled down on newly bought country estates to eat curries and prosper. If they did not have Indian servants, they had their wives and mothers cook the curries for them. When in town, they could stop at some of the coffee houses that had started serving curry meals by the late eighteenth century and have their fill of curry there.

Curries began to appear in cookery books. The first such recipe is in Hannah Glasse's *The Art of Cookery Made Plain and Easy*, published in 1747. It is hardly a curry and more of a gravy, having just a bit of roasted coriander and black pepper in it to give it an exotic flavour and a spoonful of rice for thickening. It was as if the author could just about manage to dip a tiny part of one toe in the unknown, exotic waters. In a later edition, she removed the coriander and rather boldly added turmeric, for its colour, and some ginger! So, already, there were two types of curry in Britain, a robust, almost macho one, sometimes eaten with additional chillies and swigs of Madeira, favoured by returning all-male members of the East India Company, and the 'barely there' version for the uninitiated.

During the nineteenth century, women began to join their men in India, running households with dozens of servants who cooked elaborate Indian meals on demand. Not a single dish was called 'curry' by the Indians. But the British, having already borrowed the Tamil word 'kari', meaning 'sauce', for the Indian food they ate and looking for an umbrella name to cover the variety laid out on the table, began to call all the dishes 'curry' and the entire meal 'curry and rice'. And that seems to have stuck. Queen Victoria, who had Indian servants, seems to have enjoyed her curry, though on her menus its name was written out in French!

While curry eaters with fond memories of real Indian food remained, curry for the general public in the late nineteenth and early twentieth centuries had progressed slowly from Hannah Glasse's minimalist recipe. During World War I, when thrift was called for, recipes appeared teaching housewives to perk up leftover roasts with sauces using curry powder, butter, milk, sour apples and lemon juice. Curry powder was king and could be added to soups, dressings, jellied veal and fish soufflés.

Veeraswamy's, the second major Indian restaurant to follow the Hindostanee Coffee House, opened in 1926 right off Piccadilly Circus. It was fashionable and immediately attracted royalty and nobility. By 1955, according to the *Good Food Guide*, there were nine Indian restaurants in London and four outside it.

I arrived as a student in 1957 and, soon after, witnessed the curry heavens opening up. In the 1960s and 1970s, near-identical Indian restaurants, each copying the other's menus word for word, began to spring up on every High Street. The curries were generalised, often coming from no specific region of India. Whether the restaurant owners were Pakistani, Bangladeshi or Indian, they all cooked the same things and all food was 'Indian'.

All the dishes served in these eateries were given standardised names and were assumed to have standardised amounts of heat. So korma began to represent the mildest, madras and vindaloo the hottest. In Britain, these distinctions are now firmly entrenched. I have heard a schoolboy boast, 'Oh I don't eat korma any more. I order bhuna or madras.' Indians, who make no such distinctions and who cook local dishes according to their family's tastes, would not know what this boy was talking about. Britain was creating its own British curry world that could be grasped and understood. But the curry world was to move on even as part of it stood still.

The reason for the great surge in restaurants could well have been the surge in immigrants of South Asian descent. Immigration was much easier for members of the Commonwealth before 1962. The textile mills in West Yorkshire and Lancashire were booming in the 1950s, and many Pakistanis, Kashmiris from Mirpur, took advantage of the cheaper fares to find jobs there. Those who eventually became restaurateurs, such as Mumtaz Khan of Mumtaz in Bradford and Leeds, insisted on adding their own Kashmiri spice blend, basaar mix, to the foods they served.

Many of the Punjabis who came from India settled in London's Southall, opening eateries that served parathas (pan-fried flatbreads) stuffed with potatoes, lassis (yogurt drinks) and aloo gobi, a classic made from cauliflower and potatoes.

Bengali seamen, mainly from Sylhet, had been coming to Britain since the seventeenth century as lascars for the East India Company. With the formation of Bangladesh in 1971, thousands of them poured into Britain. Today almost 90 per cent of Indian restaurants in Britain are owned by Bangladeshis, with many of them forming the staff as well. Ironically, they rarely serve Bangladeshi food. They reserve dishes such as fish balls in masala for their home cooking.

The 1960s and 1970s brought another large group of Indian immigrants, those from Africa. Rising African nationalism and resentment from leaders such as Idi Amin caused Indians who had settled in East Africa to flee. They had British passports and so most came to Britain, often in multi-generational family groups. Many Gujarati East Africans settled in the Midlands, often in the same small houses once owned by English mill workers. Today, a drive through Leicester could take you to Bobby's, which declares itself 'passionate about vegetarian food'. It serves Gujarati specialities, including one of my favourites, dal dhokri, a spicy split pea and tomato broth with fresh, handmade noodles. Drive south to Coventry to find Bimal Parmar's Gujarati-African food. Kukupaka is a delicious chicken with a coconut sauce, while mogo pili pili are cassava chips with African chilli sauce. None of these would be found in a traditional curry house.

In 1982, I made my first television series for the BBC. That same year the Bombay Brasserie opened just off Gloucester Road in London. I was cooking authentic, home-style Indian dishes for a British public that seemed very ready for them, and the Bombay Brasserie was serving very authentic regional Indian foods in an elegant club-like setting that was inviting and appealing. The public raised its arms and embraced us both.

The journey of Indian food into British hearts has been steady and almost inevitable. In this multi-cultural nation, curry today is as British as pork pies and is available any way it is desired. You want chips with curry sauce? Well, come with me to a little place in Glasgow where a Turkish manager takes some yellow powder out of a can proclaiming that the contents are 'made in China', pours it into a bucket, adds boiling water from an electric tea kettle, then mixes it all with a hand-held blender. This he pours over some fat chips.

Do you wish to see little seven-year-olds learn how to make a Kashmiri potato and spinach curry? There is an ambitious programme to bring inner-city children from Leeds and Bradford together with farming kids from the Yorkshire Dales, so they can get to know each other better. They live in bunk barns and, among other things, make each other's foods. They have already made a shepherd's pie. Now they are making a curry. Two heads, one dark, the other light, are bent over a chopping board, touching each other. Very slowly and earnestly, both children are slicing hot green chillies.

In the Curry Nation that is Britain today, you may go to a pub and order your chicken tikka masala with a pint and have the satisfaction of getting exactly what you expect, or you could go to the glamorous Cinnamon Kitchen in what was once a warehouse for the East India Company and see what modern fantasy of French techniques and Indian seasonings the chef, Vivek Singh, may conjure up for you. If you want the best of home-cooked Gujarati food, look up Gujarati Rasoi on the Internet. You will either find them in London's Borough, Broadway and Exmouth Markets or at their new restaurant.

You wish to dine at home? Indian cookery books are in every book shop and there are plenty of Asian grocers to fill up your basket with their wares. Okra, curry leaves, green chillies, ginger, tamarind paste, chickpea flour? Almost every ingredient needed for South Asian cookery is now available, sometimes imported directly from India, even batter to make dosas (pancakes) and Alphonso mangoes, the best India has to offer.

Right now a talented Bangladeshi author may be in her kitchen preparing a mustardy prawn salad (bharta) for her husband, a young, energetic Pakistani wife may be washing rice for an elaborate, saffron-inflected chicken biryani to entertain a dozen guests, a Gujarati gentleman from East Africa may be getting ready to cook up some dhora (chicken) kebabs, and a young, pretty former student may be boiling potatoes to make a delicious Nepalese potato salad with a sesame dressing for her Gurkha father.

It is the best of times for this Curry Nation. You may go out and enjoy any kind of curry your heart desires. If you wish to eat at home, remember: a lot of the recipes I have mentioned are in this book!

Appetisers, snacks and soups

Spicy chickpeas, potatoes and beans in a tamarind sauce (chana aloo chaat)

Yesmien Bagh Ali, Skipton, Yorkshire

Serves 6

Chaats are popular Indian snack foods that tantalise the taste buds with their salty, sweet and sour combination of flavours. They may be made from fruit such as guavas and star fruit (for a fruit version, see page 202), from vegetables such as sweet potatoes and potatoes, from dumplings and crispy noodles, or from boiled dried chickpeas. Here, in a modern British twist, Yesmien finds a good use for canned kidney beans and chickpeas.

Yesmien uses a bottled, shop-bought tamarind sauce. See page 192 to make your own Tamarind Chutney instead.

400g can chickpeas, drained and rinsed

400g can kidney beans, drained and rinsed

1 large potato, boiled, peeled and chopped

150g (5½oz) pomegranate seeds (optional but lovely)

1 large red onion, halved and finely sliced

2 medium tomatoes, chopped

4 tablespoons lemon juice

2 tablespoons tamarind sauce, or to taste

6 teaspoons chaat masala (ideally Yesmien's Chaat Masala, see page 216)

4 tablespoons finely chopped coriander leaves

salt, to taste

lime wedges, to serve (optional)

Put all the ingredients except the coriander leaves, salt and lime wedges into a bowl and mix gently. Taste and add salt as required.

Sprinkle the coriander leaves over the top and serve with lime wedges, if you like.

Sprouted mung bean salad

Sarojini Gulhane, London

Serves 4

This is a typically Central and North Indian dish, eaten at breakfast, lunch or just as a snack. Sarojini's mother cooked it for her brothers and sister on school days, when school started at half past seven in the morning! I remember my mother making it for breakfast on Sundays.

All sprouts are much easier to digest than the beans themselves. Unlike East Asian sprouts with long tails, South Asian sprouts have tails that have barely emerged. You can buy them from South Asian grocers, or sprout them yourself over two days.

100g (3½oz) whole, green-skinned mung beans
4 teaspoons olive or sunflower oil
½ teaspoon mustard seeds
½ teaspoon cumin seeds
½ medium onion, finely chopped
½ hot green chilli
½ teaspoon finely grated or crushed garlic
½ teaspoon peeled, finely grated root ginger
¼ teaspoon chilli powder
½ teaspoon turmeric
½–¾ teaspoon salt
1 medium tomato, finely chopped
2 tablespoons finely chopped coriander leaves
2–3 tablespoons freshly grated coconut, or frozen grated coconut, defrosted, or desiccated coconut, to garnish

Put the mung beans in a large bowl and pour over an excess of cool water. Leave to soak overnight.

Drain the beans. Spread them out on a large white plate. Carefully pick out and discard any small mung beans that have not swollen. These 'bullets', as Sarojini calls them, will remain hard and may cause alarm if chewed!

Cover the remaining mung beans with a well-dampened tea towel and leave in a dark, warm place (such as the turned-off oven) for 24 hours. Tiny shoots should emerge.

When ready to cook, set a karhai, wok or medium-sized pan, about 18 centimetres (7 inches) in diameter, over a medium heat. Pour in the oil. When it's hot, add the mustard seeds and allow them to pop for 15 seconds. Add the cumin seeds and stir and fry for a further 15 seconds, then add the onion. Sauté the onion for five minutes, or until translucent. Mix in the chilli, garlic and ginger and stir and fry for two minutes, adding a splash of water if anything threatens to stick. Stir in the chilli powder, turmeric and salt, then add the tomato and stir for one minute, or until it just starts to soften.

Tip in the mung beans and coriander and fold in gently, ensuring they are well coated in the spice paste. Cook, stirring, for two minutes. Spoon out the salad into a serving dish and garnish with the coconut to serve.

Fried savoury biscuits (matthias)

Surinder Wariabharaj, London

Serves 8

Matthias are savoury, deep-fried biscuits, generally eaten at tea time, either plain or with a sweet mango chutney. They may be flavoured with any number of spices, though the most common and traditional is carom seeds (ajwain). All Indian grocers sell these and, as they contain thymol, they taste a bit like thyme. You may substitute cumin seeds if you like.

250g (9oz) plain or matthia flour, plus more to dust
½ teaspoon salt
½ teaspoon carom seeds (ajwain)
2 tablespoons olive or sunflower oil, plus more to deep-fry

Mix all the ingredients, except the oil for deep-frying, in a large bowl, sifting the flour through your fingers to incorporate the oil, then add 6 tablespoons of water. Knead to a stiff dough.

Take a golf ball-sized piece of dough and roll it out on a floured surface to 3 millimetres (⅛ inch) thick. Then, using a sharp knife, cut into 3 centimetre (1¼ inch) strips. Make parallel cuts, at an angle to these, 1½ centimetres (¾ inch) apart, to make rhomboids. Gently gather and place on a plate. Repeat until all the dough has been used.

Pour the oil to deep-fry into a large karhai, wok or deep, sturdy pan for deep-frying and set it over a medium heat. Test to see if the oil is hot enough by dropping in a piece of dough: it should sizzle easily but not brown immediately.

Gently place a batch of biscuits – without crowding the pan – in the oil and stir gently, for three to four minutes, until light brown and puffy. Remove with a slotted spoon and drain on kitchen paper. Repeat to cook all the matthias.

Allow the biscuits to cool, then store them in an airtight container. They will keep for up to two weeks.

Onion bhajias

Nikita Gulhane, London

Serves 4

A popular snack eaten throughout India and Britain. The humble chickpea forms the basis of so many Indian dishes. In this case the flour, often called 'gram' flour or 'besan', is used to make the batter for the onion slices. Other vegetables may be used, such as slices of aubergine, cauliflower and broccoli florets, mushrooms or even chillies! They are perfect with tomato ketchup or Tamarind Chutney (see page 192).

130g (generous 4½oz)
  chickpea (gram) flour
4 tablespoons yogurt
1½ teaspoons finely grated or
  crushed garlic
1½ teaspoons peeled, finely
  grated root ginger
¾ teaspoon cumin seeds
¾ teaspoon hot chilli powder
¼ teaspoon turmeric
12 fresh curry leaves,
  shredded
4 tablespoons finely chopped
  coriander leaves
¾–1 teaspoon salt
1 large onion, halved and
  finely sliced
olive or sunflower oil,
  to deep-fry

Place the chickpea flour in a large bowl and measure in 4 tablespoons of water. Add the yogurt and beat together to create a thick paste. Add the garlic, ginger, cumin seeds, chilli powder, turmeric, curry leaves and chopped coriander. Mix well and add salt to taste. Fold the onion slices into the batter, making sure they are well coated.

Set a karhai, wok or deep, sturdy pan for deep-frying over a medium heat and pour in the oil. Test it is hot enough by dropping in a small piece of batter: it should sizzle immediately. Have a small bowl of water close to hand.

Working quickly, take small pinches of onions and, making sure they are well coated in the batter, drop three or four into the hot oil. Some will form small spidery clusters, others may separate to be individual slices. Cook the bhajias for 20–30 seconds before turning with a slotted spoon. Continue cooking for about one minute, turning occasionally, until they are a reddish-golden colour. Remove and drain in a colander.

Wet your fingers, then pick up another pinch of battered onions and repeat the process. Serve hot.

Tapioca pearl fritters (sabudana vadas)

Parul Patel, London

Makes 16

These fritters, eaten frequently during fasts in India, but great as snacks at any time, are crisp, chewy, tangy and crunchy all at once. Serve them with Parul's Green Mango, Coconut and Cashew Nut Chutney (see page 181), or any chutney of your choice. You will need to soak the tapioca pearls for five hours, so do bear this in mind when you come to make the dish.

300g (10½oz) medium-sized
    tapioca pearls
50g (1¾oz) skinless roasted
    peanuts, coarsely chopped
3 teaspoons finely chopped hot
    green chilli
3 teaspoons peeled, finely
    chopped root ginger
1 teaspoon caster sugar
1 teaspoon salt
5 teaspoons lemon juice
250g (9oz) potato, boiled and
    mashed
olive or sunflower oil, to
    deep-fry

Pour the tapioca pearls into a bowl with 300ml (10fl oz) of cold water. Cover with cling film and leave to soak for about five hours, stirring occasionally. The pearls will swell to two or three times their dried size, and should feel plump and soft when squeezed. Drain.

Mix the tapioca, peanuts, chilli, ginger, sugar and salt together. Thoroughly stir in the lemon juice. Now carefully stir in the potato, making sure there are no clumps.

Pour the oil into a large karhai, wok or deep, sturdy pan for deep-frying and set it over a medium heat. Test to see if the oil is hot enough by dropping in a tapioca pearl: it should sizzle immediately.

Wet your hands and make a ball of the tapioca mixture the size of a golf ball (about 40g/1½oz). Put the ball in one palm. Press and rotate firmly with the other palm so it becomes a patty about 6 centimetres (2½ inches) in diameter. Repeat to use up all the mixture.

Carefully place three or four of the vadas at a time in the hot oil and cook for about four minutes, carefully turning over every minute, until golden brown. Remove with a slotted spoon and drain on kitchen paper. Make all the vadas in this way. Serve hot, with chutney.

Dal fritters (dal vadas)

Chaat House, Leicester

Makes 16

These make for a great snack when eaten with tea; there has to be a dipping chutney on the side, of course! They may also be served with a meal whenever a 'crunch' is required.

This recipe is barely spiced and so the vadas may be eaten by children. If you wish to make them spicier, add 2–3 chopped hot green chillies and ¼ teaspoon cumin seeds to the dal mixture just before blending it.

The distinctive split mung dal – with pale centres and black skin – that you need is often sold as 'mung dal chilka'. You'll have to start this recipe the night before, to soak the dal.

200g (7oz) split mung dal
    (mung dal chilka)
2 tablespoons chana dal
15g (½oz) coriander leaves,
    finely chopped
2 tablespoons finely chopped
    onion
¾ teaspoon salt
olive or sunflower oil, to
    deep-fry

Pick over both dals separately and rinse them well, then soak them separately overnight in generous amounts of water. The next day, plunge your hands into the mung dal bowl and rub them between your palms to remove the skins, allowing them to float to the surface. Skim them off and repeat until they have all been removed, adding more water to the bowl if necessary. Drain both types of dal.

Add the chana dal to the mung dal and grind to a coarse paste in a blender. Transfer to a bowl and mix in the coriander, onion and salt. Take small handfuls, each about 25g (scant 1oz), and form small golf ball shapes. Flatten each in your palm to 5 centimetres (2 inches) in diameter and 2 centimetres (¾ inch) thick and arrange on a plate.

Pour the oil into a karhai, wok or deep, sturdy pan for deep-frying and set it over a medium heat. Test to see if it is hot enough by dropping in a scrap of the batter: it should sizzle immediately. Place four or five vadas in the oil and fry for two to three minutes on each side, until golden brown. Remove with a slotted spoon and drain on kitchen paper. Make all the vadas in this way. Serve hot, with chutney (try them with Tomato Chutney, see page 188).

Tapioca pearl and sweet potato fry (sabudana usal)

Sarojini Gulhane, London

Serves 4

You might describe this as a morning cereal, except that there are no grains in it and it is generally spicy. Sarojini likes to cook it on fasting days, when no grains are allowed. Her grandmother used to cook it for her and now, with its combination of fresh coconut and crunchy peanuts, it's still something of a treat. Generally, tapioca pearls are made from the tapioca or cassava root, but they can also be made from the pith inside the trunk of the sago palm. The two sources seem interchangeable. Get the medium-sized pearls.

150g (5½oz) medium-sized tapioca pearls
2 tablespoons olive or sunflower oil
1 teaspoon unsalted butter
½ teaspoon cumin seeds
10–15 fresh curry leaves, shredded
1 teaspoon finely sliced hot green chilli
2 teaspoons peeled, finely chopped root ginger
70g (scant 2¾oz) peeled sweet potato, finely chopped
3 tablespoons raw peanuts, coarsely ground
¼ teaspoon hot chilli powder
¾ teaspoon salt
4 teaspoons roughly chopped coriander leaves, plus more to garnish
freshly grated coconut, or frozen grated coconut, defrosted, to garnish

Pour the tapioca pearls into a bowl and add 150ml (5fl oz) of water. Cover with cling film and leave to soak for five hours, stirring occasionally. The pearls will swell to two or three times their dried size, and should feel plump and soft when squeezed.

Set a karhai, wok or small frying pan, about 18 centimetres (7 inches) in diameter, over a medium heat. Add the oil and butter. When the butter has melted, tip in the cumin seeds and curry leaves and allow to sizzle for 10 seconds. Mix in the chilli and ginger, stirring and frying for 10 seconds more, then stir in the sweet potato pieces and fry them for three minutes. Add the peanuts, chilli powder and salt. Stir and fry, then add the drained tapioca pearls. Gently stir and fry for three more minutes, adding most of the coriander.

Serve garnished with the grated coconut and a few more coriander leaves.

Gujarati vegetable samosas

Ranjan Davda, Leicester

Makes 12

This classic Indian snack, found over much of Britain, has many variations. This particular one comes from a Gujarati home and has a sweet and sour flavour. It is generally served with ketchup or tamarind sauce.

For the filling
200g (7oz) peeled potato, finely chopped
80g (3oz) peeled carrot, finely chopped
2 tablespoons sunflower oil, plus more to deep-fry
¼ teaspoon mustard seeds
¼ teaspoon cumin seeds
⅛ teaspoon ground asafoetida
230g (generous 8oz) frozen peas, rinsed and drained
1–2 hot green chillies, finely sliced
1 garlic clove, finely grated
½–¾ teaspoon salt
1 teaspoon ground cumin
1 teaspoon ground coriander
½ teaspoon turmeric
¼ teaspoon hot chilli powder
½ teaspoon ground cinnamon
2 tablespoons finely chopped coriander leaves
2 tablespoons lemon juice
2 teaspoons caster sugar

For the pastry
170g (scant 6oz) plain flour, plus more to dust
pinch of bicarbonate of soda
½ teaspoon salt
4 tablespoons sunflower oil

Simmer the potato and carrot until just tender. Drain. Set a medium-sized pan, about 18 centimetres (7 inches) in diameter, over a medium heat. Pour in the 2 tablespoons of oil and, when it's hot, add the mustard seeds. Allow them to pop, then add the cumin seeds and asafoetida. Stir and fry for 30 seconds, then add the potato, carrot and peas. Reduce the heat to low and cook for three to four minutes. Sprinkle in the chillies, garlic and salt, then mix in the other ingredients for the filling, tip on to a large plate and cool.

Put the ingredients for the pastry into a bowl, rubbing in the oil, then add about 4 tablespoons of lukewarm water. Knead to make a firm dough, then divide into six. Dust a work surface with flour. Take one ball and roll it into a thin 15–18 centimetre (6–7 inch) round, about 2mm (less than ⅛ inch) thick. Cut it in half with a rounded edge facing you. You now want to make a cone. Bring the left corner of the cut end towards you, folding it over just past the halfway point. Wet the outside edge of this fold. Bring over the right hand corner and tuck it 5 millimetres (¼ inch) over the left. Gently press the join together. Hold the cone open and fill with 2 tablespoons of filling, packing it to 1cm (½ inch) from the opening. Seal by wetting the edges on the inside and pressing them together. Repeat to fill all the samosas.

Set a sturdy pan for deep-frying over a medium heat and pour in the oil. Let it get very hot. Now reduce the heat to low, allow to cool for a minute, then add four samosas. Cook for one minute, turn, then cook for two minutes, turning a few times, until each side is golden. Remove and drain on kitchen paper. Increase the heat to medium-low and fry the remaining samosas in the same way.

Chicken kebabs (dhora kebabs)

Bimal Parmar, Coventry

Makes about 30

Bimal Parmar, a large man with laughing eyes, is a Gujarati, born in Mombasa, Kenya, but raised in Tanzania. He delights in serving foods of mixed heritage, as well as East African foods beloved by Indians.

He recommends Coconut Chutney (see page 182) as the ideal accompaniment to these dhora kebabs.

*2 medium onions, roughly
    chopped*
1kg (2lb 4oz) minced chicken
*300g (10½ oz) white
    breadcrumbs*
*1 tablespoon finely chopped
    garlic*
*1 tablespoon peeled, finely
    chopped root ginger*
*1 tablespoon finely chopped
    hot green chilli*
*1 tablespoon ground
    coriander*
1 tablespoon ground cumin
½ tablespoon garam masala
2 eggs, lightly beaten
2 teaspoons salt
*500ml (18fl oz) olive or
    sunflower oil*
*lime wedges, to serve
    (optional)*

Place the onions in a blender, or use a stick blender, and process them to a purée. Mix them with all the ingredients except the oil and lime wedges to form a sticky 'dough'. Using wet hands, shape into golf ball-sized patties, then flatten each to about 5 centimetres (2 inches) in diameter.

Pour the oil into a 25 centimetre (10 inch) frying pan or flat-bottomed karhai or wok and set it over a medium heat. (It will seem like a lot of oil, but in fact will come just halfway up the sides of the kebabs.) Check to see if the oil is hot enough by dropping in a small piece of the mixture: it should sizzle immediately. Now fry about six kebabs at a time for two to three minutes on each side, or until a deep golden colour.

Remove from the pan with a slotted spoon and drain on kitchen paper. Make all the kebabs in this way. Serve hot, with lime wedges, if you like.

Chilli mutton chops (chilli champ)

Suniya Quoreshi, London

Serves 6

Suniya is a busy working mum and this dish is excellent as a quick and easy starter (though do bear in mind that the meat must be marinated overnight). Mutton is readily available in most Asian butchers, but you may use lamb if you wish. Serve with a mint chutney.

Mango powder, or amchoor, is a souring agent and is sold by Asian grocers. If you cannot get it, use an extra 2 teaspoons of lemon juice instead.

1kg (2lb 4oz) mutton chops, about 1 centimetre (½ inch) thick
¾ teaspoon freshly ground black pepper
2½ teaspoons chilli flakes
½ teaspoon ground coriander
½ teaspoon ground ginger
½ teaspoon freshly ground nutmeg
¾ teaspoon amchoor (green mango powder, or see recipe introduction)
4 teaspoons finely grated garlic
1½ teaspoons peeled, finely grated root ginger
¾–1 teaspoon salt
juice of 1 lemon, plus lemon wedges to serve (optional)

Put the chops in a non-reactive bowl. Add all the other ingredients except the lemon wedges and rub well into the meat. Cover and marinate overnight in the refrigerator.

The next day, when you are ready to cook, preheat the oven to 200°C/400°F/gas mark 6. Place the chops and their marinade in a casserole dish or baking tray. Cover with a lid or foil, place in the oven and cook for 45 minutes.

Remove from the oven and turn the chops over. Add 120ml (scant 4fl oz) of water to the dish or tray to loosen the spices and create a thin sauce. Stir well, cover again and cook for a further 15 minutes. Serve the chops coated with their sticky sauce, with lemon wedges if you like.

Split pea and tomato sauce with noodles (dal dhokri)

Bobby's Restaurant, Leicester

Serves 4

This dish is a winner. The unctuously smooth noodles in a spicy tomato and toor dal sauce could seduce most mortals I know. In spite of the many ingredients, it's fairly simple to make.

South Asia has scores of noodle dishes, and this Gujarati speciality is one of them. First a soupy sauce is made with split pigeon peas (toor dal) and tomatoes, then freshly made noodles are dropped in to cook. It is hot, slightly sweet and sour and quite scrumptious. This particular recipe is from a family that came to Leicester from Uganda in East Africa.

Gujaratis serve this dal in small, individual bowls, with other vegetarian specialities, rice and breads. I like to serve it, Western-style, in old-fashioned soup plates as a starter.

For the sauce
125g (4½oz) oily or plain toor dal, washed and drained
675g (1lb 7oz) tomatoes
1 tablespoon tomato purée
2 tablespoons olive or sunflower oil
⅛ teaspoon ground asafoetida
2 hot dried chillies
2 tablespoons raw peanuts with skin (small are better)
2.5 centimetre (1 inch) cassia bark or cinnamon stick
4 cloves
¼ teaspoon mustard seeds
¼ teaspoon fenugreek seeds
10 fresh curry leaves
handful of coriander leaves
2 teaspoons lemon juice
2 teaspoons ground coriander
2 teaspoons ground cumin
¼–1 teaspoon chilli powder
1½ teaspoons garam masala
1½–2 teaspoons salt, or to taste
1½–2 tablespoons caster sugar, or to taste

For the noodles
100g (3½oz) plain flour, plus more to dust
2 tablespoons chickpea (gram) flour
1 teaspoon peeled, finely grated root ginger
¼ teaspoon very, very finely chopped hot green chillies
½ teaspoon turmeric
¼ teaspoon chilli powder
1 tablespoon sunflower oil

Recipe continued overleaf

APPETISERS, SNACKS AND SOUPS

31

First, make the sauce. Combine the dal and 475ml (17fl oz) of water in a small pan – 13 centimetres (5 inches) would be ideal – and bring to a boil. Cover partially, reduce the heat to low and cook for 45 minutes, or until the dal is tender. Meanwhile, roughly chop the tomatoes and purée them in a blender. Mash up the dal with a potato masher and mix it with the tomatoes, tomato purée and 475ml (17fl oz) more water in a bowl.

Place a larger 15 centimetre (6 inch) pan over a medium-high heat and pour in the oil. As soon as it is hot, put in the following in quick succession: first the asafoetida and dried chillies, then the peanuts, cassia and cloves, then the mustard seeds, then the fenugreek seeds and curry leaves. Now stir in the dal and tomato mixture and add all the remaining ingredients for the sauce, with salt and sugar to taste.

Bring to a boil, then stir and reduce the heat to a low simmer. Cook for 20 minutes, stirring now and then, or until the peanuts have become tender and the sauce is amalgamated. Set aside. (You could make this a day in advance, then cover and refrigerate.)

When you are preparing to eat, pour the sauce into a 15–20 centimetre (6–8 inch) pan and stir in 350ml (12fl oz) of water. Set aside.

It is best to make the noodles shortly before you eat them. Put all the ingredients in a bowl in the order listed. Mix and rub the flour with your fingertips to incorporate the oil, so it begins to look a little like coarse breadcrumbs. Slowly add about 3½ tablespoons of water, or just enough to form a dough. Work the dough for a minute, then form it into a smooth ball. Break it into three equal pieces and roll each into a smaller ball.

Flatten one ball into a patty, dip it in flour and roll it out into a 19 centimetre (7½ inch) round on a well-floured surface. With a sharp knife, first cut it lengthways into 5 centimetre (2 inch) wide strips, then across at 4 centimetre (1½ inch) intervals, to achieve stubby, rectangular noodles. Keep the pieces separated and lightly floured. Working quickly, repeat for the remaining two balls of dough.

Bring the sauce to a boil and drop in the noodles, stirring as you do so. Reduce the heat to medium-low; it should still be at a vigorous simmer. Cook, stirring now and then, for about 10 minutes, or until the noodles are just done. Serve immediately.

Lamb, pork
and beef

Lamb meatball curry (kofte)

Jagdish Kaur, Punjab'n de Rasoi, Edinburgh

Serves 6

There are no standardised recipes at Punjab'n de Rasoi. The women who cook there prepare food according to their personal preferences. Jagdish Kaur is one of the stalwarts at this unique eatery and this is her recipe. You may use low-fat minced lamb if you prefer.

Serve this on rice, or eat it with chapatis. A simple salad may be served on the side. For a fuller Indian meal, a dal and a vegetable dish may be added as well.

For the meatballs
1kg (2lb 4oz) minced lamb
1 teaspoon chilli flakes
4 hot green chillies, finely chopped
1 tablespoon peeled, finely grated root ginger
2 medium onions, finely chopped
1½ teaspoons garam masala
1 teaspoon salt
4 tablespoons chopped coriander leaves

For the sauce
5 tablespoons olive or sunflower oil

1 teaspoon cumin seeds
2 medium onions, finely chopped
6 garlic cloves, finely grated or crushed
1 tablespoon peeled, finely grated root ginger
1¼ teaspoons turmeric
2 medium tomatoes, finely chopped
4 hot green chillies, finely sliced
½ teaspoon salt
2 teaspoons garam masala
3 cloves
5 centimetre (2 inch) cassia bark or cinnamon stick
2 cassia leaves or bay leaves

Put all the ingredients for the meatballs into a large bowl. Mix well and, with wetted hands, form golf ball-sized meatballs about 4 centimetres (1½ inches) in diameter. Set aside.

To make the sauce, pour the oil into a large pan 25 centimetres (10 inches) in diameter and set it over a medium heat. When it's hot, add the cumin seeds. Let them sizzle for 10 seconds, tip in the onions and stir for eight minutes, or until they brown lightly. Stir in the garlic and ginger, loosening with a splash of boiling water if they stick. Add the turmeric and stir for one minute. Add the tomatoes and stir for two minutes, then add the chillies and salt. Stir and cook for five minutes, again adding a splash of boiling water if they stick. Add the garam masala, cloves, cassia bark and leaves and stir for two minutes.

When the oil separates, place the meatballs in the pan. Cover and cook over a low heat for five minutes. Shake the pan to loosen the meatballs. Leave for a further five minutes and shake again. The meatballs will now be firm enough to be moved. Gently rearrange them so they all have a chance to sit covered in the bubbling sauce. Pour in 250ml (9fl oz) of water, again shimmying the pan to work the liquid into the sauce. Continue cooking, covered, for 30–40 minutes over a low heat, shaking now and then, and serve.

Lamb with okra (bhindi gosht)

※ ※

Mumtaz, Leeds and Bradford

Serves 4

At Mumtaz, where the karhais (Indian woks) are lined up in long rows, they use an old-fashioned style of restaurant cooking, one much popularised by the balti houses. Most of the red meats are pre-cooked in a pressure cooker. Then, as orders come in, a quick sauce is made in a karhai, according to what a particular dish requires, the meat and some oil are added, then the sauce is cooked down until oil glistens at the edges. But Mumtaz Khan is smart: he uses his mother's Kashmiri spice mixes to enliven his food, so it tastes really good.

If you don't have a pressure cooker, bring the ingredients for the first stage to a boil with 250ml (9fl oz) of water. Cover, cook gently for 1¼–2 hours, then follow the rest of the recipe.

For the pressure cooker stage
500g (1lb 2oz) boneless lamb, in 3 centimetre
(1¼ inch) chunks
1 tablespoon peeled, finely grated root ginger
1 tablespoon roughly chopped garlic
1 medium tomato, finely chopped
2 tablespoons finely chopped onion
¼ teaspoon ground asafoetida
1 teaspoon ground coriander
3 tablespoons yogurt

For the okra
about 4 tablespoons olive or sunflower oil
300g (10½oz) okra, halved, then chopped

For the karhai stage
2 teaspoons basaar mix (ideally Yesmien's Basaar
Mix, see page 216)
½ teaspoon cumin seeds, roasted and crushed
(see page 219)
½ teaspoon ground coriander
1 medium tomato, roughly chopped
3 tablespoons yogurt
1 teaspoon dried fenugreek leaves
3 hot green chillies, sliced lengthways
1 teaspoon salt
5 tablespoons olive or sunflower oil
1 tablespoon coriander leaves, to serve

Rinse the lamb, drain and place in the pressure cooker. Mix it with the other ingredients for the pressure cooker stage, plus 120ml (4fl oz) of water, and set it over a high heat. Seal the lid and bring up to full pressure. Reduce the heat to very low and cook for 30 minutes. Turn off the heat and allow the pressure to drop. Now for the okra. Pour half the oil into a large frying pan, karhai or wok. Add half the okra. Sauté for up to four minutes, or until all stickiness has been cooked away. Remove and drain on kitchen paper. Cook the second batch in the same way.

To finish the dish, empty the pressure cooker into a large karhai or wok and bring to a boil. Add the okra and all the ingredients for the karhai stage except the coriander leaves. Mix well. Cook over the highest heat for 10–11 minutes, stirring gently from the bottom. Add 120ml (4fl oz) of water if you want more sauce. It is ready when the oil separates. Spoon off as much oil as you desire, then transfer to a warmed serving dish and garnish with the coriander.

Lamb with potatoes (aloo gosht)

Saleem Zahid, London

Serves 4

This dish, prepared by Saleem, is in the style of his family; they came to Pakistan from Aligarh in northern India. It is a very comforting, home-style dish, perfect both for the family and for entertaining. You will need to get your butcher to chop the lamb up on the bone.

Serve with flatbreads, simple salads and a raita. Saleem likes to make a salad to serve with it: chopped onions and tomatoes dressed with vinegar, salt and green chillies.

4 tablespoons olive or
    sunflower oil
2 medium onions, halved and
    finely sliced
1 black cardamom pod
6 green cardamom pods
4 centimetre (1½ inch) cassia
    bark or cinnamon stick
8 cloves
1 tablespoon finely grated or
    crushed garlic
1 tablespoon peeled, finely
    grated root ginger
600g (1lb 4oz) bone-in lamb
    shoulder, cut into 2.5
    centimetre (1 inch) chunks
1 teaspoon salt
1 whole nutmeg, grated
1 teaspoon chilli powder
1 teaspoon garam masala
1 teaspoon ground cumin
2 teaspoons ground coriander
250ml (9fl oz) yogurt
500g (1lb 2oz) potatoes, peeled,
    cut into large chunks

Pour the oil into a medium-sized pan, about 23 centimetres (9 inches) in diameter, and set it over a medium heat. Add the onions and sauté for five minutes. Now sprinkle in both types of cardamom pod, the cassia bark and cloves. Continue to brown the onions with the whole spices for a further five minutes. Stir in the garlic and ginger and brown for two or three minutes more, pouring in a splash of boiling water if the paste begin to stick.

Now add the meat, stir several times and add half the salt. Continue to seal the meat for 10 minutes. Tip in the grated nutmeg and mix well. Add the chilli powder, garam masala, ground cumin and coriander. Reduce the heat to low and pour in the yogurt. Combine well.

Increase the heat to medium-high, browning the meat with the yogurt. Stir in the potatoes with the remaining salt and 370ml (13fl oz) of water. Bring to a boil, cover, reduce the heat to low and cook for 50 minutes, or until everything is tender, then serve.

Lamb with beetroot (chukandar gosht)

Saleem Zahid, London

Serves 3–4

In very Muslim tradition, meat is prepared with all manner of vegetables. Here it is cooked with grated beetroot, which lend a gentle sweetness to the dish.

Saleem's grandmother, who came from Aligarh in India, taught him that when he was cooking with a vegetable he should add slightly more cumin than coriander. If he were to cook just meat, he would need to use more coriander than cumin. He has steadfastly followed this advice.

Serve with flatbreads or rice. A green vegetable may be added, as can a dry potato curry, dal and raita. You will need to ask a butcher to chop up the meat on the bone for you.

*4 tablespoons olive or
  sunflower oil
2 medium onions, halved and
  finely sliced
1 tablespoon finely grated or
  crushed garlic
1 tablespoon peeled, finely grated
  root ginger
500g (1lb 2oz) bone-in lamb
  shoulder, cut into 2.5 centimetre
  (1 inch) chunks
1 large black cardamom pod
2.5 centimetre (1 inch) cassia
  bark or cinnamon stick
½ teaspoon chilli powder
1 teaspoon garam masala
1½ teaspoons ground cumin
1 teaspoon ground coriander
1 teaspoon salt
375g (13oz) beetroot, peeled
  and coarsely grated
2 medium tomatoes, roughly
  chopped*

Pour the oil into a large non-stick karhai, wok or pan, about 25 centimetres (10 inches) in diameter, and set it over a medium heat. Add the onions and stir and fry for about 10 minutes, until brown. Spoon in the garlic and ginger and continue to brown for two or three minutes, splashing in a little boiling water if the paste starts to stick to the base. Add the lamb, increase the heat, and turn to seal on all sides for five minutes.

Reduce the heat to low and add the black cardamom, cassia bark, chilli powder, garam masala, ground cumin and coriander. Mix well and cook, stirring occasionally, for 10 minutes.

Add half the salt, stir well, then mix in the beetroot and tomatoes. Increase the heat and mix well for four to five minutes, until the tomatoes begin to soften. Add the remaining salt and stir. Reduce the heat to low, cover and cook for 50 minutes, or until the meat is tender, stirring occasionally and adding a splash of boiling water if needed to maintain the juiciness in the pan. Serve.

Lamb browned in its sauce (lamb kosha)

Mallika Basu, London

Serves 4

Mallika is young and pretty. She has a blog in which she discusses her rushed life as the working mother of two small children, with many tips on cooking for her family. To hurry things along, she uses a pressure cooker, which is commonly used throughout India to save time and fuel. If you do not have one, follow this general recipe using a wide, heavy-based pan. Once the meat has browned, add 250ml (9fl oz) of water and bring to a boil. Cover, reduce the heat to low and cook gently for 1¼–2 hours, or until the meat is very tender, adding a little more hot water if it is drying up. Once it is tender, follow the rest of the recipe.

Mallika is originally from Bengal and uses a very Bengali technique to get caramelisation into the sauce: she adds sugar to the oil when she starts cooking.

For the marinade and meat	For the sauce
500g (1lb 2oz) lamb neck fillet, cut into 2 centimetre (¾ inch) chunks	2 tablespoons olive or sunflower oil
1 teaspoon turmeric	1 teaspoon caster sugar
1 teaspoon ground cumin	1 medium onion, roughly chopped
1 teaspoon ground coriander	1 teaspoon finely grated or crushed garlic
1 teaspoon salt	1 teaspoon peeled, finely grated root ginger
1½ teaspoons olive or mustard oil	1 teaspoon chilli powder
2 tablespoons Greek yogurt	4 tomatoes, quartered
	1 teaspoon garam masala

Combine the meat with all the marinade ingredients in a non-reactive bowl, mix well, cover and leave in the refrigerator for at least four hours, or overnight.

Pour the oil for the sauce into a pressure cooker (or see the recipe introduction) and set it over a medium heat. When it's hot, add the sugar and stir occasionally for one minute as it dissolves. Add the onion and sauté for 30 seconds, then stir in the garlic and ginger. Fry for 10 minutes, or until the onion is browned. Spoon in the chilli powder and mix well. Increase the heat to medium-high and add the tomatoes. Cook for one minute, then add the meat and its marinade. Brown the meat well on all sides for six to seven minutes. The tomatoes and meat will release plenty of juices. Mix, then seal the lid. Heat to full pressure. Reduce the heat to very low and cook under pressure for 20 minutes. Turn off the heat and allow the pressure to drop by itself.

Open the lid and return the pan to a high heat. Bring to a boil and add the garam masala. Stir for 10 minutes to reduce the sauce, until it is thick and the oil separates, then serve.

Lamb with whole spices (khara masala gosht)

Ismet Ahmed, London

Serves 4

This is spring lamb cooked with whole, aromatic spices such as cinnamon, cardamom and cloves. It is cooked in yogurt, which lends a gentle tartness. If spring lamb is unavailable, use any other lamb. You will need to ask a butcher to chop up the meat on the bone for you. Serve with a dal and flatbread.

4 tablespoons olive or
*   sunflower oil*
4 medium onions, finely sliced
1 teaspoon salt
500g (1lb 2oz) bone-in spring
*   lamb shoulder, chopped*
*   into 2.5 centimetre*
*   (1 inch) chunks*
2 tablespoons finely grated or
*   crushed garlic*
2 tablespoons peeled, finely
*   grated root ginger*
4 hot dried chillies
4 green cardamom pods
2 x 2.5 centimetre (1 inch)
*   pieces cassia bark or*
*   cinnamon stick*
5 cloves
15 whole black peppercorns
375g (13oz) yogurt

Pour the oil into a medium-sized pan, 23–25 centimetres (9–10 inches) in diameter, and set it over a medium heat. Take half a sliced onion and brown it for about seven minutes. Add the salt, stir, then add the meat. Sear and seal the meat for three minutes before adding all the remaining ingredients.

Incorporate thoroughly, cover and cook over a medium heat for one hour, stirring occasionally.

Now uncover and continue to cook until the oil separates, leaving the meat juicy but without sauce. Serve.

Kashmiri-style rich lamb curry

Yesmien Bagh Ali, Skipton, Yorkshire

Serves 4

Here is a dark lamb curry, cooked in a Kashmiri style. Yesmien has a kettle of hot water ready as she cooks it, and keeps adding small splashes to her spices and seasonings as they brown. This prevents them from burning and helps her to create a wonderfully burnished sauce. Again, as the lamb pieces contain bones, get your butcher to chop them for you.

As accompaniments, serve a dal, such as Red Lentil and Chana Dal (see page 138) and any vegetable dish, such as Potato and Spinach Curry (see page 120). Serve with rice or flatbreads.

6 tablespoons olive or sunflower oil

2 medium onions, halved and finely sliced

8 garlic cloves, finely grated or crushed

2 cassia leaves or bay leaves

2 black cardamom pods, lightly crushed

5 centimetre (2 inch) cassia bark or cinnamon stick

1 teaspoon cumin seeds

2.5 centimetres (1 inch) peeled, finely grated root ginger

2 medium tomatoes, roughly chopped

1 hot green chilli, roughly chopped

1 tablespoon shop-bought basaar mix or other Kashmiri spice mix (ideally Yesmien's Basaar Mix, see page 216)

1½ teaspoons salt

75g (2¾oz) coriander leaves and stems, finely chopped

750g (1lb 10oz) bone-in lamb from the shoulder, leg or both, cut into 2.5 centimetre (1 inch) chunks

1 teaspoon garam masala

Pour the oil into a large pan, about 25 centimetres (10 inches) in diameter, and set it over a medium-high heat. Tip in the onions. Stir and fry for 15 minutes, until brown. Add the garlic and fry for one minute more. Splash in a tablespoon of hot water and stir it in. Let it disappear. Stir in the cassia leaves, cardamom pods, cassia bark and cumin seeds. Add the ginger and stir and fry for 30 seconds, then tip in the tomatoes. Mix in 3 tablespoons of hot water, cover and cook for four minutes, stirring occasionally. Sprinkle in the chilli and combine, then add the basaar mix and salt, with a tablespoon of hot water. Stir and fry for five minutes. As you do so, the oil will begin to separate from the paste.

Now add half the coriander and mix well for one minute. Drop the meat into the pan and brown well all over for 10 minutes. Pour in 750ml (1½ pints) of hot water, cover and simmer over a low heat for one hour, stirring occasionally.

Add the garam masala, mix well, replace the lid and keep cooking gently for 10 minutes. Fold in the remaining coriander before serving.

Pakistani lamb curry

Lahore Kebab House, London

Serves 6

This is Head Chef Mohammed Azeem's recipe for a simple, very traditional lamb curry. It is cooked with young, bone-in spring lamb at Lahore Kebab House, a popular, Pakistani-style London eatery; that is the way most South Asians prefer their meat curries. (You will need to get your butcher to chop the meat for you.) A couple of marrow bones are always added to improve the flavour and texture of the sauce. Use the youngest lamb you can find and cook it until it is tender. Older lamb will, of course, take longer to cook.

I found it very amusing that the staff at this restaurant know that most Westerners do not care for bones, so they keep a good portion of the marrow bones for themselves. After they have cooked them, they devour the marrow as a well-deserved treat!

You could garnish this dish with coriander leaves and more peeled root ginger matchsticks, if you like. Serve with chapatis or a rice dish.

250ml (9fl oz) olive or sunflower oil
450g (1lb) onions, finely sliced
1½ teaspoons cumin seeds
1 teaspoon chilli powder
1 teaspoon freshly ground black pepper
1 teaspoon turmeric
2 teaspoons salt
6 hot green chillies, or fewer as desired, finely chopped
5 centimetres (2 inches) root ginger, peeled and cut into matchsticks
4 garlic cloves, roughly chopped
2 medium tomatoes, roughly chopped
1.5kg (3lb 5oz) bone-in lamb shoulder, cut into 3 centimetre (1½ inch) chunks
180ml (6fl oz) yogurt

Pour the oil into a large, deep pan, about 25 centimetres (10 inches) in diameter, and set it over a medium heat. When it's hot, add the onions. Stir and cook for about 10 minutes, or until they are dark brown.

Add the cumin seeds, chilli powder, black pepper, turmeric and salt. Stir and cook for a further two minutes, then add the green chillies, ginger, garlic and tomatoes. Cook for a few minutes, or until the tomatoes start to break up.

Now increase the temperature to high, add the lamb pieces and brown them for 10 minutes. Mix in the yogurt, then pour in 1 litre (1¾ pints) of warm water and bring to a simmer. Stir, reduce the heat to low, cover and cook for 40–60 minutes, or until the meat is tender.

Uncover, increase the heat to high and boil away some of the liquid, so you are left with a generous puddle of sauce. Spoon off any excess oil, if desired, and serve.

Braised lamb shanks (nihari)

Lahore Kebab House, London

Serves 4 generously

Here is a very Muslim recipe, frequently eaten as a holiday breakfast dish after prayers. At the Lahore Kebab House it is offered in the evenings as well, to a very grateful clientèle.

While I was watching this dish being prepared, I was wondering what spices they would use to give the distinctive nihari flavour. Much to my surprise, I saw the chef open a packet of spice mix and add it to the pot! In fact in many South Asian households this is what people do, especially given the pace of life. You may do so if you wish, using a whole packet of nihari spice mix. However, I find it is just as easy to grind the spices myself and that is what I have done for this recipe.

In many Muslim homes, nihari is reserved for special occasions, and much enjoyed with naans or other flatbreads.

For the nihari
4 lamb shanks, total weight about 2kg
   (4lb 8oz)
salt, to taste
120ml (4fl oz) olive or sunflower oil
15 centimetre (6 inch) piece root ginger, peeled
   and coarsely chopped
1 whole nutmeg, crushed into smaller pieces
1 tablespoon mace blades
2 tablespoons fennel seeds
3 cassia leaves or bay leaves, shredded
2.5 centimetre (1 inch) cassia bark or
   cinnamon stick, broken into small pieces
1 teaspoon ground ginger
1 teaspoon black peppercorns
1 teaspoon nigella seeds
1 teaspoon cloves
2 teaspoons cumin seeds
45g (scant 1¾oz) unsalted butter
1 medium onion, sliced into rings
1 tablespoon paprika
1 teaspoon hot chilli powder
2 tablespoons wholemeal flour or
   chapati flour

For the garnish
4 tablespoons fine julienne of peeled root ginger
2–3 hot green chillies, finely sliced
handful of coriander leaves
lemon wedges

Recipe continued overleaf

First there is a little preparation to do. Place the lamb shanks on a plate and rub with ½ teaspoon of salt and a little of the oil. Set aside. Now put the ginger in a blender with 5 teaspoons of water and process to a fine paste. Set aside separately. Place the nutmeg, mace, fennel seeds, cassia leaves, cassia bark, ground ginger, peppercorns, nigella, cloves and cumin seeds in a clean coffee grinder or spice grinder and grind to a fine powder. Set this aside, too.

Preheat the oven to 160°C/325°F/gas mark 3.

Put a large flameproof casserole dish with a tight-fitting lid, about 30 centimetres (12 inches) in diameter, over a medium heat and add the butter. When it has melted, sprinkle in the onion and fry for about five minutes, until brown. Remove with a slotted spoon.

Now pour the remaining oil into the pan. When it's hot, put in the shanks two at a time and, turning with a pair of tongs, brown each side for two minutes. Remove. Repeat with the other shanks.

Working quickly, reduce the heat to low and add the ginger paste. Stir continuously for four or five minutes until light brown. Then add the paprika and chilli powder and stir for one minute, followed by the ground spice mixture and 1½ teaspoons of salt. Mix well thoroughly to infuse the oil. Add the browned onions, stir, then pour in 1.2 litres (2 pints) of warm water. Mix well, then arrange the shanks in the pan. Cover and place the casserole in the centre of the oven. Leave to cook for three hours, basting and turning the shanks every 30 minutes.

Remove the pan from the oven and uncover. Carefully lift out the shanks into a large, warmed serving bowl. Spoon off as much excess oil from the cooking liquid as possible. Check the sauce for seasoning and adjust as necessary. Set the casserole over a low heat.

Mix the flour slowly with 4 tablespoons of water to achieve a thin paste. Stir the paste into the sauce, cooking for five to six minutes to thicken, then pour it over the meat in the serving bowl.

Serve all four garnishes in little bowls on the table for diners to add to the nihari as they like.

Curried lamb's kidneys

Suniya Quoreshi, London

Serves 4–6

Kidneys and all other innards are commonly eaten throughout Pakistan. This is a fairly quick and simple dish to prepare. Suniya likes to serve it with flatbreads and salad or raita. You may also serve it with rice, and vegetables such as Potato and Long Bean Curry (see page 122).

*4 tablespoons olive or
  sunflower oil
2 medium onions, finely
  chopped
5 hot green chillies, halved
  and deseeded
¾ teaspoon cumin seeds
¾ teaspoon turmeric
¾ teaspoon ground coriander
¾ teaspoon freshly ground
  black pepper
¾ teaspoon chilli flakes
1⅓ tablespoons tomato purée
1kg (2lb 4oz) lamb's kidneys,
  quartered
3 medium tomatoes, peeled
  and finely chopped
2 teaspoons finely grated or
  crushed garlic
2 teaspoons peeled, finely
  grated root ginger
1½ teaspoons salt
30g (1oz) coriander leaves,
  chopped*

Set a large frying pan, about 23 centimetres (9 inches) in diameter, over a medium heat. Pour in the oil. When it's hot, add three-quarters of the onions and cook until barely golden, about five minutes. Add the chillies and stir and fry, then tip in the cumin seeds, turmeric, ground coriander, black pepper, chilli flakes and tomato purée, with a splash of water. Stir gently.

Now put in the kidneys and increase the heat to high to seal the kidneys and make them paler. Stir and fry for two minutes, then tip in the tomatoes. Cook for four minutes, stirring. Add the garlic, ginger and salt, stir a few times, then cook for three minutes.

Add the coriander leaves and the remaining onion. Stir and cook for one minute, to reduce the sauce, then serve.

Rogan josh shepherd's pie

❀ ❀

Vivek Singh, The Cinnamon Club, London

Serves 6–8

This recipe, served at Vivek's restaurant Cinnamon Soho, is an amalgamation of two very popular dishes, one from North India and the other from Britain. You can make individual pies or one large pie.

I suggest a lovely green salad on the side.

For the rogan josh filling
3 tablespoons olive or sunflower oil
2 red chillies
1 teaspoon cumin seeds
4 cloves
2 bay leaves
2 green cardamom pods
1 black cardamom pod
2 tablespoons finely chopped garlic, plus
  2 teaspoons finely grated garlic
2 medium onions, finely chopped
1¼ teaspoons salt, or to taste
2 teaspoons peeled, finely grated root ginger
500g (1lb 2oz) boneless leg of lamb, cut into
  1 centimetre (½ inch) chunks
2 teaspoons chilli powder
2 teaspoons ground coriander
2 teaspoons ground cumin
2 tablespoons tomato purée
700g (1lb 9oz) minced lamb
2 tablespoons yogurt
2 teaspoons garam masala (ideally Vivek's
  Garam Masala, see page 214)
15g (½ oz) coriander leaves, chopped

For the mashed potatoes
800g (1 lb 12oz) floury potatoes, peeled and
  roughly chopped
¼ teaspoon turmeric
¼ teaspoon salt
1–2 tablespoons unsalted butter, to taste
50g (1¾oz) cheddar or parmesan cheese, grated

Pour the oil into a large, shallow, heavy-based flameproof casserole dish about 30 centimetres (12 inches) in diameter and 7½ centimetres (3 inches) deep and set it over a medium-low heat. Add the whole spices and stir and fry for 30 seconds.

Add the chopped garlic and fry for 30 seconds, until it starts to brown. Tip in the onions and ¼ teaspoon of the salt and sauté for 10 minutes, until soft. Now add the grated garlic and ginger and the lamb chunks. Stir and fry for 10 minutes, sealing the meat. Now add the chilli powder, ground coriander and cumin and ½ teaspoon more salt and stir well. Measure in the tomato purée and add the minced lamb and yogurt. Sauté for another 10 minutes. Add 240ml (scant 9fl oz) of water plus ¼ teaspoon more salt and bring to a boil. Reduce the heat to low, cover and cook gently for 25 minutes. Preheat the oven to 200°C/400°F/gas mark 6.

Add the garam masala to the lamb and stir to mix. Cover and cook for a final five minutes, adding ¼ teaspoon more salt if required.

Meanwhile, prepare the potatoes. Cook them in boiling water, with the turmeric and salt, for 20–25 minutes, or until soft. Drain and add the butter and cheese. Mash to a consistency you like.

Fold the coriander leaves into the lamb mixture, then dot tablespoons of the potatoes on top and spread out with the back of a fork (or make individual pies, if you wish, in small ovenproof dishes). Place in the oven for 10 minutes, or until brown and bubbling, then serve.

Gurkha-style pork curry with choi sum

❧❧❧❧❧❧❧❧❧❧❧❧❧❧❧❧❧❧❧❧❧❧❧❧❧❧❧❧❧❧❧❧

Adapted from Pemba Lama, Basingstoke

Serves 6

Pemba is a Sherpa, which means that he belongs to the clan that came originally from Tibet and seemingly took over aspects of the mountaineering business in Nepal. He is also a gurkha, which is the name given to all Nepalese who join an army.

One of the common customs for gurkha regiments is to have 'messing huts'. These are usually outdoors and are places for social gatherings where soldiers can drink, eat, dance and generally relax. Large pots are set up inside the messing hut. Foods such as accompanying dals and vegetables may be brought in from the barracks but special meats, such as pork, are always cooked inside the hut by one or more soldiers. This pork dish happens to be much loved by the gurkhas of the British army.

The Chinese green, choi sum, is added to the stew just before the cooking finishes. Other similar greens such as bok choi may be used instead.

The normal choice of cut here is pork belly, but Pemba tells me that pork shoulder is also well liked. Most gurkhas like their meat to be fairly resistant to the tooth, but I have cooked it a little longer for those of us who are used to tender meat!

For the spice paste
1 teaspoon cumin seeds
1 teaspoon coriander seeds
4 green cardamom pods
2.5 centimetre (1 inch) cinnamon stick
2 hot dried chillies

For the pork
3 tablespoons mustard oil
¼ teaspoon fenugreek seeds
½ teaspoon carom seeds (ajwain)
½ teaspoon cumin seeds
2 medium onions, finely sliced
2 teaspoons finely grated garlic
2 teaspoons peeled, finely grated root ginger
1 teaspoon turmeric
½ teaspoon chilli powder
2 bay leaves
1kg (2lb 4oz) boneless pork shoulder, cut into
*   2.5 centimetre (1 inch) chunks*
2 medium tomatoes, finely chopped
1 teaspoon tomato purée
1¼ teaspoons salt
1 hot green chilli, sliced lengthways
2 hot red chillies, sliced lengthways
2 tablespoons dark soy sauce
1 small lemon, cut into 8 pieces, seeds removed
250g (9oz) choi sum, stems cut into 3, leaves shredded

Recipe continued overleaf

Grind the spices for the paste to a coarse powder in a clean coffee grinder or spice grinder, adding three to four teaspoons of water to make a paste.

Set a large pan, about 25 centimetres (10 inches) in diameter, over a medium-high heat. Pour in the oil and, when it's hot, add the fenugreek seeds. Allow to darken for five seconds, then add the carom and cumin seeds. Swirl the pan for 20 seconds, then tip in the onions.

Reduce the heat to medium and stir and fry the onions for three to four minutes until lightly coloured. Add the garlic and ginger, turmeric, chilli powder and bay leaves. Stir and fry for one minute, then spoon in the spice paste. Mix well for two minutes, then add the meat, increase the heat to medium-high and brown well on all sides for 10 minutes.

Pour in 240ml (9fl oz) of boiling water and cover, reducing the heat to medium and shaking the pan occasionally. After 25 minutes, add another 240ml (9fl oz) of boiling water, stir and cover. After 15 minutes further, add 120ml (4fl oz) of boiling water and stir. Cover for five more minutes, then add the tomatoes and tomato purée. Add the salt, stir it in, then follow with the green and red chillies and the soy sauce. Cook for two minutes, then add the lemon chunks. Mix well, then fold in the choi sum. Continue to cook, uncovered, for five more minutes until the greens are done, then serve.

Goan pork vindaloo with potatoes

❧❧❧❧❧❧❧❧❧❧❧❧❧❧❧❧❧❧❧❧❧❧❧❧❧❧❧❧❧❧❧

Serves 4

A classic from my *Ultimate Curry Bible*, this dish is such a favourite with the British that I have to include it here. You could think of this recipe as 'vindaloo light'. It has the garlic, vinegar, black pepper and chillies – in this case chilli powder – that a vindaloo requires, but in gentle quantities. Serve it with plain rice.

You could also choose to make this in a pressure cooker. To do so, follow the general recipe, but add just 120ml (4fl oz) of water, bring to full pressure, then reduce the heat to very low and cook for 17–20 minutes (20 minutes will give very tender meat).

2 teaspoons mustard seeds
1 teaspoon cumin seeds
2 teaspoons coriander seeds
3 cloves
1 medium onion, roughly
    chopped
5 garlic cloves, chopped
2½ centimetre (1 inch) root
    ginger, peeled and chopped
2 tablespoons cider vinegar
¾–1 teaspoon chilli powder
2 teaspoons paprika
salt, to taste
½ teaspoon turmeric
½ teaspoon freshly ground
    black pepper
560g (1lb 4oz) boneless
    pork shoulder, cut into 2½
    centimetre (1 inch) chunks
3 tablespoons olive or
    sunflower oil
340g (scant 12oz) waxy red
    potatoes, peeled and cut the
    same size as the pork
½ teaspoon caster sugar

Put half the mustard seeds and all the cumin seeds, coriander seeds and cloves in a clean coffee grinder or spice grinder and grind as finely as possible.

Tip this spice mixture into a blender with the onion, garlic, ginger, vinegar, chilli powder, paprika and 3 tablespoons of water. Blend until smooth.

Rub 1¼ teaspoons of salt, all the turmeric, black pepper and 2 tablespoons of the spice paste all over the pork. Put in a plastic food bag, seal and marinate in the refrigerator for at least 30 minutes, or longer if desired.

Pour the oil into a large, heavy-based, non-stick, lidded pan and set it over a medium-high heat. When the oil is hot, add the remaining mustard seeds. As soon as they pop, which will be in a matter of seconds, put in the remaining spice paste. Stir and fry for five to six minutes, or until the paste is lightly browned. Put in the pork with its marinade and stir for a minute. Cover and reduce the heat to medium. Let the meat cook for about 10 minutes, lifting the lid now and then to stir; it should become lightly browned.

Now pour in 750ml (1½ pints) of water and add the potatoes, ½ teaspoon of salt and the sugar. Stir and bring to a boil. Cover, reduce the heat to low and cook very gently for 50–60 minutes or until the meat is tender, then serve.

Minty beef meatballs (pudinay vale kofte)

Sumayya Jamil, London

Serves 4

Sumayya has her own individual approach to cooking. She is demanding of herself and very thorough. Her meatballs are unusual. She grinds her beef very fine, makes the meatballs larger than most and adds a lovely mint flavour. Serve these with rice or chapatis. A dal and vegetable would complete the meal.

For the meatballs
1 tablespoon chickpea (gram) flour
500g (1lb 2oz) minced beef
1 teaspoon ground coriander
½ teaspoon cumin seeds
1 teaspoon garam masala
¾ teaspoon chilli powder
1 teaspoon salt
½ teaspoon finely grated or crushed garlic
½ teaspoon peeled, finely grated root ginger
15g (½oz) coriander leaves, finely chopped
3 mint leaves, shredded
½–1 green chilli, finely chopped

For the onion and poppy seed pastes
3 tablespoons olive or sunflower oil
2 small onions, sliced
2 tablespoons poppy seeds

For the sauce
3 tablespoons olive or sunflower oil
1 teaspoon cumin seeds
1 teaspoon ground coriander
½ teaspoon turmeric
½ teaspoon chilli powder
½ teaspoon salt
1 teaspoon Kashmiri (mild) chilli powder
120g (scant 4oz) yogurt
12 mint leaves

First roast the chickpea flour in a dry frying pan, stirring, until it turns a shade darker and smells nutty. Scrape out on to a plate and set aside.

Now make the onion paste: pour the 3 tablespoons of oil into a small pan and fry the onions until they are nicely brown all over. Remove with a slotted spoon and process as finely as possible in a blender. For the poppy seed paste, soak the seeds in hot water to cover for 10 minutes, then drain and crush finely in a mortar and pestle. Set aside.

Make the meatballs: put all the ingredients, plus 1 tablespoon of the onion paste, into a food processor. Process until they are well blended. Remove and form into smooth meatballs, each about 4 centimetres (1½ inches) in diameter, using wetted palms.

Now to make the sauce: pour the oil into a large, shallow pan, about 25 centimetres (10 inches) in diameter, and set it over a medium heat. Add 2 tablespoons of onion paste and brown for two or three minutes. Reduce the heat to low and add the cumin seeds, coriander, turmeric, chilli powder and salt. Mix well and add a splash of boiling water if the spices stick. Spoon in all the poppy seed paste and the Kashmiri chilli powder. Stir and fry until the oil separates and the sauce is cooked.

Stir in the yogurt and then add 180ml (6fl oz) of hot water. Mix well and cook for three minutes. Add the meatballs, cover and cook over a low heat for 30 minutes. Tear the mint leaves and add to the sauce. Stir gently to mix them in, and serve.

Eggs and chicken

Egg curry

Saumya Singh, London

Serves 2

Saumya works for a bank. She loves to cook and often serves this very simple curry to her friends. Its tomato and onion sauce may also be served over fish or with – yes – chips! This curry may be eaten with chapatis or other flatbreads, or served on toast.

4 medium tomatoes (about 450g/1lb) roughly chopped
1 medium onion, roughly chopped
2 tablespoons olive or sunflower oil
4 eggs
1 tablespoon ground coriander
1 teaspoon garam masala
½ teaspoon chilli powder
1 teaspoon turmeric
¾ teaspoon salt, or to taste
handful of chopped coriander leaves

First, reduce the tomatoes to a purée in a blender, or with a stick blender. Separately, do the same to the onion.

Pour the oil into a small, preferably non-stick pan, about 15 centimetres (6 inches) in diameter, and set it over a medium-high heat. When it's hot, put in the onion paste. Stir and fry for eight to 10 minutes, or until it is lightly browned. Add the tomatoes, stir well, then cover. Continue to cook for another 10 minutes, stirring carefully now and then as the tomatoes will splutter. Meanwhile, bring a saucepan of water to a boil, lower in the eggs (a large spoon is useful here) and boil for eight minutes. Drain and plunge into cold water to stop the cooking, then peel the eggs and halve them lengthways.

Back to the sauce: when it has reduced and is not spluttering as much, add the ground spices and salt. Stir and cook for another minute. Now add 250ml (9fl oz) of water and the coriander leaves, cover and bring to a boil. Cook for two to three minutes over a medium heat.

Lay the halved eggs carefully in the sauce, spooning some of it over them. Cook over a low heat, uncovered, for a final two to three minutes, then serve.

Green masala minced chicken (hare masala ka chicken keema)

Saleem Zahid, London

Serves 4–6

Saleem likes to eat this for brunch with large, shop-bought naans. He even likes to stuff the chicken into a hollowed-out bread roll, topped with finely sliced onion.

4 tablespoons olive or sunflower oil
2 medium onions, finely chopped
1 tablespoon finely grated or crushed garlic
1 tablespoon peeled, finely grated root ginger
700g (1lb 9oz) minced chicken, ideally thigh meat
1¼ teaspoons salt
4–6 hot green chillies, finely sliced
½ teaspoon turmeric
3 tablespoons lemon juice
75g (2¾oz) coriander leaves, finely chopped

Set a karhai, wok or large pan (whichever you use, it must have a lid), about 25 centimetres (10 inches) in diameter, over a medium heat. Pour in the oil. When it's hot, add the onions and sauté for five to six minutes, until light brown and soft. Add the garlic and ginger. Stir and fry for two to three minutes.

Add the minced chicken and increase the heat to medium-high. Stir and fry for five to six minutes, ensuring all the morsels of meat turn white. Add the salt, chillies, turmeric, lemon juice and chopped coriander and incorporate thoroughly, stirring for two minutes.

Cover, reduce the heat to low and cook for 15–20 minutes. Taste for balance of seasonings, making adjustments if needed, then serve.

Chicken in a wok (karhai chicken)

Mumtaz, Leeds and Bradford

Serves 4

This is a typical karhai (formerly balti) dish prepared at Mumtaz restaurants in woks set over very, very high heat. The stoves in the kitchens here noisily shoot out vertical jets of flame like the tail ends of rockets, allowing the staff to cook very quickly.

The curries are made in an almost upside down manner: the oil is added after the ingredients are practically cooked. This technique relies on a very high cooking heat to dry off the cooking liquids, leaving just the oil to brown the meats and seasonings.

1 medium tomato, peeled and roughly chopped, plus 1 more, quartered

500g (1lb 2oz) boneless, skinless chicken thighs, cut into 2½ centimetre (1 inch) chunks

1½ tablespoons finely chopped onion

3 tablespoons peeled, finely grated root ginger

1½ tablespoons finely grated garlic

4 tablespoons yogurt

¼ teaspoon ground asafoetida

1 teaspoon salt

1 tablespoon basaar mix (ideally Yesmien's Basaar Mix, see page 216)

1 teaspoon ground coriander

1 teaspoon ground cumin

5 tablespoons olive or sunflower oil

With a stick blender, blend the roughly chopped tomato to a purée.

Mix the chicken, blended tomato, onion, ginger, garlic, 3 tablespoons of the yogurt, the asafoetida and salt in a karhai, wok or medium-sized pan, about 23 centimetres (9 inches) in diameter. Set it over the highest heat you can muster and bring to a boil.

Cook, stirring and mixing, for five to six minutes. Add the basaar mix, ground coriander and cumin and stir for one minute.

Pour in the oil, incorporate thoroughly and cover for one minute. Uncover and stir in the tomato quarters and remaining yogurt. Stir for another two minutes, or until all signs of the yogurt have disappeared and the oil has pooled at the surface. Serve.

Chicken in a coconut sauce (kukupaka)

Bimal Parmar, Coventry

Serves 2

Bimal is a Gujarati from East Africa. He loves the foods from East Africa, and cooks Indian, African and mixed dishes. This is a mixed dish. 'Kuku' means chicken and 'paka' is coconut. Serve it with rice and vegetables.

For the marinade
1 teaspoon finely chopped hot green chilli
1 teaspoon peeled, finely chopped root ginger
1 teaspoon finely grated or crushed garlic
¼ teaspoon salt

For the rest
2 whole chicken legs, skinned, scored 3 or 4
 times across both thigh and drumstick
3 tablespoons olive or sunflower oil, plus more
 for the chicken
6 tablespoons very finely chopped red onion

1½ teaspoons crushed or finely grated garlic
1½ teaspoons peeled, finely grated root ginger
1 teaspoon finely chopped hot green chilli
1 medium tomato, finely chopped
¼ teaspoon ground cumin
¾ teaspoon ground coriander
½ teaspoon turmeric
¼ teaspoon chilli powder
¼ teaspoon salt, or a bit more, to taste
250ml (9fl oz) coconut milk, from a well-shaken can
1 lime, cut into 4, to serve
a few coriander leaves, to serve

Mix all the marinade ingredients together and rub well into and over the chicken legs in a non-reactive container, making sure to go into the slits. Refrigerate for at least an hour.

When you're ready to cook, preheat the oven to 200°C/400°F/gas mark 6. Lightly brush the chicken with oil, then place on a baking tray. Slide the tray into the middle of the oven and cook for 30–40 minutes, or until done. (Pierce the thickest thigh to check: the juices should run clear with no trace of pink. Cook for a little longer if needed.) Remove from the oven and rest for five minutes.

Meanwhile, put the 3 tablespoons of oil into a medium-sized frying pan, about 20 centimetres (8 inches) in diameter, and set it over a medium heat. When it's hot, add the onion, frying for about five minutes or until the pieces brown at the edges. Add the garlic, ginger and green chilli. Stir for a minute. Add the tomato and cook until soft, about three minutes. Add the ground cumin and coriander, the turmeric, chilli powder and salt, stirring all the while. Mix in the coconut milk and bring to a boil. Cook rapidly over a medium-high heat, stirring, until the sauce thickens a bit. Place the chicken in the sauce to heat through, spooning the sauce over it. Remove from the heat. Take the chicken pieces out, put them on a warmed serving plate and pour the sauce over the top. Serve with the lime wedges and garnish with the coriander.

Chicken with cream (chicken malaidar)

Mister Singh's India, Glasgow

Serves 4–5

There are now three generations of this particular Singh family in Scotland. At their flagship restaurant, Mister Singh's India in Glasgow, the male youngsters working as staff wear kilts and tartan ties, topped with turbans, of course, as they are all Sikhs. Their accents are Scottish and their common names, emblazoned on their lapel badges, are all Western. Bobby Singh from the middle generation explained that their aim is to cater to what the Scots want, so they have taken to producing curry pies – which do very well at football games – and forms of Indianised haggis, such as haggis pakoras and haggis curry, served on top of fried flatbreads called padoras (or bhaturas in most of India, see page 164). The haggis, in this case, comes conveniently from a can.

This, one of the dishes on their menu, is certainly not for the faint of heart: it is full of cream and butter. This is not at all unusual in the Punjab, where Sikhs originated. It is a farming and dairy state where even everyday dishes include ghee, butter, buttermilk, thickened yogurt and cream. There is also spinach in the dish. The head chef, Barry Singh, likes to use canned, puréed spinach, as he says it works best.

The restaurant uses chicken breast for this recipe. You may do so if you wish. I used boned and skinned thighs, as I find them more juicy. Serve this with rice or Indian breads.

6 tablespoons olive or sunflower oil

350g (12oz) onion, finely chopped

1 teaspoon cumin seeds

2 tablespoons finely grated garlic, plus
    2 garlic cloves, finely chopped

2 tablespoons peeled, finely grated root ginger

2 teaspoons salt

1 teaspoon hot chilli powder

1 tablespoon finely chopped hot green chilli,
    plus 2 hot green chillies, sliced, to garnish

680g (1lb 7oz) boneless, skinless chicken thighs, cut
    into 4 centimetre (1½ inch) chunks

200ml (7 fl oz) single cream

880g can puréed spinach

2 tablespoons unsalted butter

4 tablespoons finely chopped coriander leaves

2 teaspoons garam masala

2 tablespoons dried fenugreek leaves (kasuri methi)

Set a large pan, about 28 centimetres (11 inches) in diameter, over a medium heat. Pour in the oil and, when hot, add the onion. Stir and fry for one minute, then add the cumin seeds. Continue to stir and fry for about 10 minutes, or until the onion is light brown.

Add the grated garlic and the ginger, stirring until the garlic no longer smells raw, then measure in the salt and stir. Now add the chilli powder and half the finely chopped green chilli. Mix well for one minute, then add the chicken. Increase the heat to medium-high and stir for five minutes, allowing it to colour a little on all sides.

Pour in half the cream and cook on a gentle bubble for one minute, then mix in the spinach and stir for two minutes. Add the remaining cream and cook for five minutes.

Mix the chopped garlic with the butter, then drop in this garlic butter, mix, and add the remaining finely chopped green chilli. Cook for two minutes, then add half the chopped coriander and the garam masala. Continue to stir and cook for another two minutes, crumbling in the dried fenugreek leaves. Mix well, reduce the heat to low and cook for two more minutes. Sprinkle with the sliced chillies and remaining coriander, then serve.

Chicken with spinach (chicken palag)

Zahda Saeed, London

Serves 6

Zahda asks her butcher to skin and chop the chicken into 12 pieces. No bones are removed. This is a simple Punjabi version of a classic dish, generally eaten with rice or flatbreads, a yogurt relish and a simple salad of onions, tomatoes and cucumbers.

*6 tablespoons olive or
     sunflower oil*
3 medium onions, finely sliced
6 garlic cloves, peeled
400g can plum tomatoes
1 teaspoon hot chilli powder
½ teaspoon turmeric
4 teaspoons ground coriander
2 teaspoons ground cumin
2 teaspoons garam masala
1–1½ teaspoons salt
*2 teaspoons peeled, finely
     grated root ginger*
*1.2kg (2lb 12oz) whole
     chicken, skinned and
     chopped into 12 pieces*
*450g (1lb) frozen spinach,
     thawed and finely chopped*
4 tablespoons whole milk
2 whole green chillies

Set a large pot, about 25 centimetres (10 inches) in diameter, over a medium heat. Add the oil and, when it's hot, tip in the onions and whole garlic cloves. Stir and fry for a few minutes, then cover. Cook for 15 minutes until brown, stirring occasionally and adding a splash of water, if necessary.

Increase the heat to high and add the plum tomatoes and a little of the juice from the can. Stir and mash for two to three minutes. Add the chilli powder, turmeric, ground coriander and cumin and the garam masala, mashing until you have a thick sauce. Mix in the salt and ginger.

Put in the chicken pieces and brown them on all sides for two to three minutes. Cover and cook over a low heat for 15 minutes, stirring occasionally. Increase the heat to high and add the spinach, milk and chillies. Mix well and cook over a medium heat for 15–20 minutes, stirring now and then and adding small amounts of water if the chicken seems to stick or brown too much. Serve.

Madhur's chicken tikka masala

Serves 4–6

Probably created in Britain, chicken tikka masala – or CTM as it is often called – is easily the most popular Indian curry in the UK today. Marks & Spencer claim to sell 18 tonnes of it every week; an estimated 23 million portions are sold in Indian restaurants each year; while 10 tonnes a day are produced by Noon products, to be sold in supermarkets.

And yet nobody is quite clear about its origins. It is possible that a chef in Birmingham, with too many tandoor-roasted chicken pieces ('tikkas') left over, decided to reheat them in a quick stir-fried curry sauce. However it originated, it is here to stay.

The tikkas need to marinate for six to eight hours, so bear that in mind when you come to make the dish. Serve CTM with Indian breads or rice. A black dal would go well with such a meal. I prefer chicken thighs but you may use breasts if you wish.

For the chicken tikka
675g (1lb 7oz) boneless, skinless chicken
    thighs or breasts, cut into 2½ centimetre
    (1 inch) chunks
1¼ teaspoons salt
3 tablespoons lemon juice
1 tablespoon peeled, finely grated root ginger
2 garlic cloves, finely grated or crushed
1 teaspoon ground cumin
1 teaspoon paprika
½–¾ teaspoon chilli powder
6 tablespoons whipping cream
½ teaspoon garam masala
3 tablespoons olive or sunflower oil

For the masala
4 tablespoons olive or sunflower oil
140g (5oz) onions, halved and finely sliced
1 tablespoon peeled, finely grated root ginger
5–6 garlic cloves, crushed
1 tablespoon ground coriander
½ teaspoon turmeric
¾ teaspoon chilli powder
2 teaspoons paprika
4 tablespoons yogurt
2 medium tomatoes, peeled and very finely chopped
350ml (12fl oz) chicken stock
¼ teaspoon salt, or to taste
¼ teaspoon garam masala
4 tablespoons chopped coriander leaves

Recipe continued overleaf

Start by marinating the chicken tikka. Put the chicken in a non-reactive bowl and rub in the salt and lemon juice. Prod the chicken pieces lightly with the tip of a knife and rub the seasonings in again, then set aside for 20 minutes. Add the ginger, garlic, cumin, paprika, chilli powder, cream and garam masala. Mix well, cover, and refrigerate for six to eight hours (longer will not hurt).

When you're ready to cook, make the masala: pour the 4 tablespoons of oil into a large, preferably non-stick, lidded pan and set it over a medium-high heat. When the oil is hot, put in the onions. Stir and fry until they brown, six or seven minutes. Add the ginger and garlic and continue to fry, stirring, for a minute. Add the ground coriander, turmeric, chilli powder and paprika. Stir for 10 seconds, then add a tablespoon of the yogurt. Stir and fry until it is absorbed. Add the remaining yogurt in this way, a tablespoon at a time.

Now put in the tomatoes. Fry them for three or four minutes, or until they turn pulpy. Add the stock and salt, and bring to a simmer. Cover, reduce the heat to low, and simmer gently for 15–20 minutes. The sauce should turn thick. Stir in the garam masala and coriander leaves, taste for balance of seasonings and add more salt if you need it.

Shortly before you eat, preheat the grill to its highest setting. Thread the chicken on to two to four skewers (the flat, sword-like ones are best). Brush with the 3 tablespoons of oil and balance the skewers on the rim of a shallow baking tray, so that the meat is suspended and does not touch the tray. Place about 13 centimetres (5 inches) from the source of heat and grill for six minutes on each side, or until lightly browned, cooked through and charred in places. (Cut a large piece of chicken to the centre to check there is no trace of pink.)

When the tikkas are cooked, reheat the sauce and fold in the chicken. Serve immediately.

Fenugreek chicken (methi chicken)

Balwinder Kaur, Punjab'n de Rasoi, Edinburgh

Serves 4–6

A simple dish, good with both rice and chapatis.

4 tablespoons olive or sunflower oil
1 medium onion, finely chopped
1 teaspoon finely grated or crushed garlic
1 teaspoon peeled, finely grated root ginger
700g (1lb 9oz) boneless, skinless chicken thighs, cut into 2½ centimetre (1 inch) chunks
4 tablespoons roughly chopped canned tomatoes
3–4 hot green chillies, finely chopped
½ teaspoon salt
1 teaspoon turmeric
¼ teaspoon chilli powder
1 teaspoon garam masala
1½ tablespoons dried fenugreek leaves (kasuri methi)

Set a 25 centimetre (10 inch) pan over a medium heat. Add the oil and, when it's hot, tip in the onion. Stir and fry for 10 minutes, or until it is light brown, then add the garlic and ginger. Stir and fry for two minutes.

Now add the chicken and brown for two minutes. Put in the tomatoes and green chillies. Stir for two minutes, then add the salt and turmeric. Mix well for five minutes before adding the chilli powder and garam masala. Stir and crumble in the dried fenugreek leaves. Mix in 360ml (13fl oz) of hot water, or enough just to cover the chicken, and bring to a simmer. Cover and cook over a low heat for 20 minutes, then serve.

Pan-roasted whole chicken with carom seeds

Sumayya Jamil, London

Serves 4–6

Here is a chicken marinated overnight in a yogurt spice mix, then cooked in a pan. Serve it with rice and a side dish of beans, okra, or dal.

For the chicken
1.5kg (3lb 5oz) whole chicken, skinned
2 tablespoons lemon juice
1 tsp coarse sea salt
3 tablespoons olive or sunflower oil

For the marinade
500ml (18fl oz) yogurt
2 tablespoons ground coriander
1 tablespoon ground cumin
½ teaspoon carom seeds (ajwain)
1 teaspoon chilli flakes
¼ teaspoon turmeric
2 tablespoons olive or sunflower oil
½ teaspoon salt
½ teaspoon peeled, finely grated root ginger
½ teaspoon finely grated or crushed garlic

For the garnish
2 tablespoons finely chopped coriander leaves
1 lemon, cut into wedges

Rub the chicken with the lemon juice and the coarse sea salt. Tie the legs together as you do when roasting. Place it in a large, non-reactive container.

Combine all the ingredients for the marinade and use it to coat the chicken inside and out. Cover, and marinate overnight.

Heat the 3 tablespoons of oil in a large, deep pan with a lid, about 30 centimetres (12 inches) in diameter, and set it over a medium-high heat. Put the whole chicken in and fry it, turning it over to seal all sides for four to five minutes. (Use a pair of tongs, gripping half inside the cavity and half out, to manipulate the chicken.) Pour in the remaining marinade from the container and reduce the heat to low.

Cover and cook for about 1¼ hours, or until done. (Test by inserting a skewer into the thickest part of the thigh, between the leg and the body. If the juices run clear with no trace of pink, it is cooked. Continue to cook for a little longer if needed.)

Remove the chicken from the pan and place on a warmed serving dish. Reduce the remaining juices to create a thick gravy. Pour these juices back over the chicken and garnish with the chopped coriander and lemon wedges.

Whole roasted masala chicken

Serves 4–6

This is my Sunday roast chicken. I serve it with Roasted Masala Potatoes (see page 121).

For the marinade
4 tablespoons lemon juice
2 tablespoons peeled, finely chopped
  root ginger
2 tablespoons finely chopped or crushed garlic
3 hot green chillies, finely chopped
1 teaspoon salt
2 tablespoons olive or sunflower oil
1 teaspoon ground cumin
1 teaspoon ground coriander
1 teaspoon garam masala (ideally My Garam
  Masala, see page 214)

For the chicken
1.75kg (3lb 14oz) whole chicken, skinned
½ teaspoon chilli powder
½ teaspoon freshly ground black pepper

Preheat the oven to 200°C/400°F/gas mark 6.

Place all the marinade ingredients in a blender and process to a paste.

Using a sharp knife, make two deep, diagonal cuts into each breast of the chicken, going all the way down to the bone. Make two equally deep slashes in the thighs and two in the drumsticks as well. Place the chicken, breast side up, on a roasting tray lined with enough foil to cover the bird completely. Pour the marinade paste over the chicken, rubbing it well into all the cuts. Set aside for 30 minutes.

Sprinkle the chilli powder and black pepper over the chicken evenly. Wrap up the chicken in the foil so it is completely covered, with the tightly closed seam at the top. Bake in the middle of the hot oven for one hour. Unwrap, without letting the juices run out, and cook, uncovered, for 15 minutes, basting two or three times with the juices.

Check the chicken is cooked by inserting a skewer into the thickest part of the thigh, between the leg and the body. If the juices run clear with no trace of pink, it is cooked. Continue to cook for a little longer if needed.

Set the chicken in a warm place to rest for 10–15 minutes, then carve and serve.

Nagore chicken curry

Ganapati Restaurant, London

Serves 4–6

At Ganapati, this dish, a creation of one of the chefs from Nagore in Tamil Nadu, is usually made with guinea fowl, which he was fond of poaching. You may use one if you so wish. At the restaurant, they make their spice paste with fresh grated coconut. You can buy that frozen these days, or use desiccated unsweetened coconut instead.
Serve with Coconut Rice (see page 143).

For the spice paste
4 tablespoons freshly grated coconut
1 tablespoon cumin seeds
1 tablespoon coriander seeds
1 teaspoon fenugreek seeds
1 teaspoon black peppercorns
4 dried chillies
20–30 fresh curry leaves

For the curry
6 tablespoons olive or sunflower oil
3–4 green chillies

6 finely grated or crushed garlic cloves
1 tablespoon peeled, finely grated root ginger
2 medium red onions, halved and finely sliced
2 medium white onions, halved and finely sliced
½ teaspoon turmeric
3 medium tomatoes, finely chopped
2 teaspoons salt
1 whole chicken, about 1.6kg (3½lb), skinned and
    portioned into 10 pieces (drumsticks, thighs,
    wings and halved breasts)
120ml (scant 4fl oz) coconut milk
4 tablespoons finely chopped coriander leaves

For the spice paste, set a karhai, wok or small frying pan, about 18 centimetres (7 inches) in diameter, over a medium heat and add the coconut, stirring until it browns. Add the cumin, coriander and fenugreek seeds, the peppercorns and dried chillies. Continue to stir for two or three minutes. As the spices release their aromas, drop in the curry leaves. Stir for 30 seconds, then cool. Grind in a clean coffee grinder or spice grinder to a fine, slightly oily powder.

To make the curry, set a large pan, about 25 centimetres (10 inches) in diameter, over a medium heat. When it's hot, pour in the oil. Drop in one whole green chilli. Stir and allow the skin to blister for 30 seconds. Add the garlic and ginger. Stir and fry for two to three minutes, until the garlic just starts to brown. Tip in the onions and sauté for 16–18 minutes, until soft and golden. Add splashes of boiling water to prevent any sticking. Stir in the turmeric. Tip in the spice paste and incorporate thoroughly for one or two minutes. Now add the tomatoes and cook, covered, for about 10 minutes. Stir occasionally, mashing the tomatoes into the sauce and reducing the heat if the tomatoes seem to catch. Add the remaining green chillies, slit lengthways, and the salt. Mix well, then add the chicken. Brown the meat for about 10 minutes. Pour in 400ml (14fl oz) of water and combine well. Add the coconut milk and coriander. Stir, cover and cook over a low heat for about 35 minutes, or until done.

Fish and seafood

Goan prawn curry

Aileen Fernandes, London

Serves 6–8

Aileen is a Goan who came to London via Zimbabwe. When she wrote to her mother for recipes, this is the prawn curry she was sent. Serve it with plain rice and the Mango Salsa she has created for it while living in London (see page 181).

2 tablespoons olive or
 sunflower oil
1 medium onion, finely
 chopped
1 teaspoon finely chopped
 garlic
1 tablespoon ground cumin
2 tablespoons chilli powder
1 1/3 tablespoons ground
 coriander
1/2 teaspoon salt
2 x 400ml cans coconut milk,
 well shaken
2 teaspoons tamarind
 concentrate
3 small stock cubes (Aileen
 used Maggi chicken cubes)
4 teaspoons caster sugar,
 or to taste
750g (1lb 10oz) raw king
 prawns, peeled and
 de-veined
2 hot green chillies, sliced
 lengthways

Pour the oil into a non-stick karhai, wok or large pan, about 25 centimetres (10 inches) in diameter, and set it over a medium heat. Put in the onion and brown for about five minutes. Add the garlic and fry for a further three minutes, then tip in the cumin, chilli powder, coriander and salt. Reduce the heat and mix well for one minute. Pour in the coconut milk and spoon in the tamarind concentrate, then crumble in the stock cubes and add the sugar.

Bring to a boil, then reduce the heat to a simmer. Reduce the sauce until it is thick. Mix in the prawns and chillies and cook for two to three minutes until the prawns are just opaque and cooked through, then serve.

Hot Punjabi king prawn curry

Jagdish Kaur, Punjab'n de Rasoi, Edinburgh

Serves 4

There is an overnight marinating required here, so plan ahead. This simple curry may be served with shop-bought naan or with rice, and it goes well with green coriander chutney. You may wish to add a vegetable dish to the meal.

For the marinade
600g (1lb 4oz) raw king prawns, peeled and de-veined
6 tablespoons yogurt
2 hot green chillies, finely sliced
½ teaspoon salt

For the curry
4 tablespoons olive or sunflower oil
½ teaspoon cumin seeds
2 medium onions, finely chopped
1 tablespoon finely chopped or crushed garlic
1 teaspoon turmeric
2–3 hot green chillies, finely sliced
2 teaspoons garam masala
½ teaspoon salt
2 medium tomatoes, roughly chopped
½ teaspoon chilli flakes
4 teaspoons finely chopped coriander leaves

Rinse and drain the prawns. Pat them dry and put into a non-reactive bowl. Add the yogurt, chillies and salt. Mix well, cover and marinate overnight in the fridge.

When ready to cook the curry, pour the oil into a karhai, wok or heavy-based pan, about 23 centimetres (9 inches) in diameter, and set it over a medium heat. Spoon in the cumin seeds, swirl and brown for 10 seconds. Add the onions. Sauté for about 10 minutes or until brown all over. Add the garlic, reduce the heat to low and stir and fry for two minutes. Mix in the turmeric and stir for one minute.

Now add the green chillies, increase the heat to medium and stir for one minute. Mix in 1½ teaspoons of the garam masala and stir for one minute. Add half the salt, and all of the tomatoes and chilli flakes. Cook for two minutes, then add 120ml (4fl oz) of boiling water. Combine to make a thick sauce.

Simmer for three minutes, then add the remaining salt. Stir in the prawns and their marinade and cook over a medium heat until they are just opaque and cooked through. Sprinkle the remaining garam masala over the top and stir. Fold in the chopped coriander and serve.

Prawn curry with spinach

Lutfun Hussain, London

Serves 4

Lutfun is a wonderful gardener. She grows vegetables at a public farm within the City of London, and does her utmost to encourage the Bangladeshi community around her to eat simple, nourishing meals. She does this partly through regular cooking classes. Here is one of the dishes in her repertoire.

3 tablespoons olive or sunflower oil
2 garlic cloves, finely slivered
1 medium onion, halved and finely sliced
1 medium tomato, peeled and finely chopped
½ teaspoon turmeric
½ teaspoon ground cumin
½ teaspoon ground coriander
½ teaspoon mild Madras curry powder
½ teaspoon salt
1 teaspoon hot green chillies, finely chopped
250g spinach, washed and shredded
450g (1lb) raw king prawns, peeled and de-veined
2 spring onions, finely sliced
6 tablespoons finely chopped coriander leaves

Pour the oil into a karhai, wok or large frying pan and set it over a medium heat. When it's hot, put in the garlic. Stir once, then add the onion. Stir and fry for about four minutes, or until light brown. Add the tomato and cook for two to three minutes, or until soft. Now add the ground spices, salt and green chillies. Stir a few times and add 120ml (4fl oz) of water.

Cover, reduce the heat to low and cook for two minutes. Now add the spinach and stir. Cover and let the leaves wilt completely.

Uncover and add the prawns and spring onions. Stir and cook over a medium heat for three to five minutes, or until the prawns are just opaque and cooked through. Add the chopped coriander and mix in to serve.

Fish balls in masala (fish kofte)

Tahmima Anam, London

Serves 4–6

Bangladeshis love their fish, which, traditionally, are collected from the fresh waters of lakes, ponds, estuaries and rivers. The fish are cooked in thousands of different ways, with kofte or 'meatballs' being just one of them. Tahmima, a renowned novelist, whose first novel, A Golden Age, caused a well-deserved sensation, lives in London and loves to cook Bangladeshi food, often following her mother's recipes. This is a dish she and her mother cooked for us.

Instead of Bangladeshi fish, many of which are now available in London, frozen, she used coley, which she said was perfect for these. Do not substitute another fish. Tahmima would serve this with rice and a dry okra dish (see Dry Okra, page 115).

For the kofte
600g (1lb 4oz) fresh coley, skinned and finely chopped
1 slice of white bread, soaked in water, squeezed and finely chopped
1 small potato, peeled and very finely chopped
1 tablespoon very finely chopped onion
1 tablespoon peeled, very finely chopped root ginger, plus 1 teaspoon peeled, finely grated root ginger
1 tablespoon finely chopped coriander leaves
1 teaspoon ground cumin
½ teaspoon finely grated or crushed garlic
½ teaspoon ground cinnamon
1 teaspoon salt

For the sauce
4 tablespoons olive or sunflower oil
6 tablespoons finely ground red onion (processed to a paste in a blender)
1 tablespoon peeled, finely grated root ginger
1 teaspoon finely grated or crushed garlic
1½ teaspoons ground cumin
½ teaspoon turmeric
½ teaspoon chilli powder
¾ teaspoon salt
125g (4½oz) canned chopped tomatoes
2 tablespoons coconut milk

Place all the ingredients for the kofte in a large bowl and combine thoroughly. Roll into balls about 4 centimetres (1½ inches) in diameter.

Now for the sauce. Set a karhai, wok or large pan, about 25 centimetres (10 inches) in diameter, over a medium heat. Pour in the oil and, when it's hot, add the onion paste. Stir and fry for two minutes until it starts to turn translucent. Add the ginger and garlic. Stir and fry for two minutes. Add the cumin, turmeric, chilli powder and salt. Stir for one minute, then add the tomatoes. Cook for two minutes, then spoon in the coconut milk and 120ml (4fl oz) of water. Bring to a boil, then reduce to a simmer.

Place the fish balls in the sauce. Cook for 10 minutes, turning them occasionally, then serve.

Boatman's curry

Serves 4

I got this recipe from a boatman who served it to his passengers in the waterways of Kerala. He'd caught the fish from the lake he was sailing; it was the popular flat fish called 'karimeen'. This was cleaned and cut across into two or three pieces, head and all. You may do the same to a flat fish such as plaice, or use steaks from any firm-fleshed fish, such as cod or salmon.

For the spice paste

4–6 dried hot chillies, soaked in hot water for 15 minutes, then drained
1 teaspoon chilli powder
3 tablespoons ground coriander
1 tablespoon paprika
1 teaspoon turmeric
115g (4oz) freshly grated coconut, or frozen grated coconut, defrosted

For the curry

2 teaspoons tamarind concentrate
3–4 hot green chillies, halved lengthways
2.5 centimetre (1 inch) piece peeled root ginger, lightly crushed
4–5 very small shallots, peeled and lightly crushed
1 ½ teaspoons salt
750g (1lb 10oz) fish steaks, about 1 centimetre (½ inch) thick (or see recipe introduction)

Put all the ingredients for the spice paste into a blender. Add 120ml (4fl oz) of water and blend to a smooth paste.

Scrape the spice paste into a medium-sized heavy-based pan. Add 120ml (4fl oz) more water and stir. The paste should have a similar consistency to puréed soup.

Place the pan over a medium-low heat and bring to a gentle simmer. Add the tamarind, green chillies, ginger, shallots and salt. Stir and simmer for two to three minutes.

Now slip in the fish, stir once and cover. Simmer gently for 10–15 minutes, until the fish is just cooked, then serve.

Seared halibut with Bengal dopiyaza sauce

Vivek Singh, The Cinnamon Club, London

Serves 4

Vivek Singh is the proud owner of three classy fusion restaurants: The Cinnamon Club, Cinnamon Kitchen and Cinnamon Soho. Here is one of his creations, a modern fish dish served at Cinnamon Kitchen. Oddly enough, this restaurant is in a building that used to be a warehouse for the East India Company, storing all the spices of India.

This dish is a meal unto itself, made in several parts. I would serve it with crusty French or Italian bread.

For the marinade
½ teaspoon nigella seeds
½ teaspoon fennel seeds
1 dried chilli, coarsely shredded
1 teaspoon salt
1 tablespoon olive or sunflower oil

For the fish and sauce
4 x 175g (6oz) halibut fillets, patted dry
1 tablespoon mustard oil
3 tablespoons olive or sunflower oil
1 bay leaf
½ teaspoon nigella seeds
½ teaspoon fennel seeds
1 onion, finely sliced
½ teaspoon peeled, finely grated root ginger
½ teaspoon finely grated garlic
½ teaspoon chilli powder
½ teaspoon turmeric
1 medium tomato, finely chopped
1 tablespoon grain mustard
250ml (9fl oz) fish stock or water
3 hot green chillies, slit lengthways
1 teaspoon salt if using water, ½ teaspoon
   if using stock
½ teaspoon caster sugar
¼ teaspoon garam masala
1 teaspoon finely chopped coriander leaves
250ml (9fl oz) coconut milk

For the red onion garnish
2 tablespoons unsalted butter
1 large red onion, finely sliced
¼ teaspoon nigella seeds
¼ teaspoon fennel seeds
¼ teaspoon salt
¼ teaspoon caster sugar
½ tablespoon white wine vinegar
juice of ½ lemon

For the spinach
1 tablespoon olive or sunflower oil
2 teaspoons finely chopped garlic
1 teaspoon cumin seeds
200g (7oz) baby leaf spinach

Recipe continued overleaf

Mix all the marinade ingredients in a small, non-reactive bowl, then rub gently over the fish fillets. Set aside for 15 minutes. Preheat the oven to 200°C/400°F/ gas mark 6.

For the sauce, heat the mustard oil with 1 tablespoon of the olive or sunflower oil in a medium-sized pan, about 20 centimetres (8 inches) in diameter. Place over a medium-high heat. Tip in the bay leaf, nigella and fennel seeds, stir and fry for five seconds, then add the onion. Sauté for five minutes until golden brown, then add the ginger and garlic. Reduce the heat to low and add the chilli powder and turmeric. Stir and fry for three minutes, then mix in the tomato. Stir and cook for four to five minutes, then spoon in the mustard. Mix well for three minutes, then pour in the stock and bring to a simmer. Add the green chillies, salt, sugar, garam masala and coriander leaves. Pour in the coconut milk, stir and simmer until reduced to a thick sauce.

Set a large ovenproof pan, about 25 centimetres (10 inches) in diameter, over a medium heat. Pour in the remaining 2 tablespoons of oil and, when it's hot, put in the fish fillets, skin side down. Hold them down firmly to ensure a good contact, or they will curl up. Sear for three to four minutes, then carefully turn over for two minutes. Transfer the pan to the hot oven for six to eight minutes.

Meanwhile, prepare the red onion garnish and spinach. For the onion, set a medium-sized frying pan, about 25 centimetres (10 inches) in diameter, over a medium heat, and melt the butter. Add the red onion and sauté until soft. Sprinkle in the nigella and fennel seeds and salt. Stir, then add the sugar. Pour in the vinegar and lemon juice, stir again and remove from the heat.

To cook the spinach, set a karhai or wok over a medium-high heat and heat the oil. Add the chopped garlic and stir and fry until it starts changing colour. Add the cumin seeds and fry for 30 seconds, or until the garlic is light brown. Tip in the spinach and stir for 15–30 seconds, until all the leaves have wilted.

Spoon the sauce into deep warmed plates, then add a layer of spinach. Place the halibut on top and garnish with the tangy red onion rings.

Keralan fish curry

Adapted from Ganapati Restaurant, London

Serves 4

The Ganapati Restaurant in Peckham specialises in South Indian food and Claire Fisher, the head chef and owner, is not even Indian. She has just come to love the food, travelling to India to learn more about it. She employs a jolly bunch of South Indian chefs, however.

Her restaurant makes this dish with kingfish. In India it would be fresh, in Britain it is generally frozen. Use it only if is of good quality, otherwise use a tuna loin, fresh salmon, prawns or fresh mackerel fillets. The restaurant uses kodampuli, also known as fish tamarind. I have only seen this ingredient in Kerala. It is the skin of a small mangosteen-like fruit which is preserved by smoking. It adds both sourness and smokiness to the dish. If you can find it, rinse four pieces of kodampuli and add them after the sauce has cooked for 50–55 minutes. In this version I have used the much more readily available tamarind concentrate.

2 medium onions, halved and finely sliced
1 red onion, halved and finely sliced
40–50 fresh curry leaves
3 hot green chillies, slit but left whole
15g (½oz) peeled root ginger, cut into fine
  julienne
2 large tomatoes, each cut into 8 wedges
1½ teaspoons chilli powder
½ teaspoon turmeric
1 tablespoon ground coriander
1 tablespoon tomato purée

4 tablespoons olive or sunflower oil
½ teaspoon fenugreek seeds
2 teaspoons tamarind concentrate
1½ teaspoons salt
400g can coconut milk, well shaken
2 tablespoons desiccated coconut
2 teaspoons coconut oil
800g (1lb 12oz) boneless 5 centimetre (2 inch)
  chunks of kingfish (or see recipe introduction)

Place both types of onion, half the curry leaves, the chillies, ginger, tomatoes, chilli powder, turmeric, ground coriander and tomato purée in a large bowl. Mix in 750ml (1½ pints) of water. Set a large pan, about 25 centimetres (10 inches) in diameter, over a medium heat. Heat the oil and, when it's hot, drop in the fenugreek seeds. Stir and fry for a few seconds until they turn light brown. Pour in the onion and tomato mixture. Cook, partially covered, for 50–55 minutes. Stir occasionally, mashing the tomatoes into the sauce.

Now add the tamarind concentrate and stir, cooking uncovered for 10 minutes. Add the salt. Pour in the coconut milk and desiccated coconut. Mix well. Add the remaining curry leaves and the coconut oil. Bring to a boil, then reduce the heat to a simmer. Place the fish in the pan and poach in the sauce until just cooked through. Serve.

Fish in a Bengali-style sauce (macher jhol)

Roti Chai Restaurant, London

Serves 3–4

Cod fillets would flake apart in this curry but cod loin, handled gently, works perfectly. If you cannot get it, it might be best to shift to firmer seafood. Salmon or prawns would work well.
Normally, a mustard sauce known as kasundi is added to give that special taste that Bengalis love. As it is hard to find, I use grain mustard. Fish stock is salty, so taste as you go.

For the marinade
2 teaspoons ground coriander
½ teaspoon turmeric
¼ teaspoon salt
1 tablespoon lemon juice
½ teaspoon Kashmiri or other mild red chilli powder

For the fish
450g (1lb) cod loin, cut into 4 centimetre (1½ inch) chunks
6 tablespoons mustard oil
12 cauliflower florets
½ teaspoon nigella seeds
3 hot green chillies, sliced
1 teaspoon crushed garlic
2 teaspoons peeled, finely grated root ginger
2 medium onions, chopped
2 teaspoons grain mustard
1½ teaspoons ground coriander
1½ teaspoons turmeric
2 teaspoons Kashmiri or other mild red chilli powder
4–5 tablespoons tomato passata
3 fish stock cubes
2 tablespoons chopped coriander leaves

Mix together all the ingredients for the marinade. Coat the cod chunks in the marinade and leave for five minutes.

Set a large frying pan over a medium-high heat and pour in 2 tablespoons of the mustard oil. Allow it to smoke. Carefully fry the fish all over for one or two minutes, just allowing the chunks to firm up. Remove and drain on kitchen paper. Place the cauliflower in the same oil. Stir and fry for two minutes, until brown all over. Remove and place in a bowl. Cover with cling film and allow to sweat.

Put a karhai, wok or large pan, 25 centimetres (10 inches) in diameter, over a medium heat. Pour in the remaining mustard oil. When it's hot, add the nigella seeds, chillies, garlic and ginger. Stir for two minutes, until lightly brown. Increase the heat to high and add the onions. Fry for two minutes. Reduce the heat to medium and add 120ml (4fl oz) of water. Mix well and cover. Cook the onions for 10–12 minutes until soft and brown, stirring occasionally. Add the mustard and stir in the ground coriander, turmeric and chilli powder. Stir uncovered for one minute, then add the tomato passata. Combine thoroughly.

Now pour in 250ml (9fl oz) of water. Dissolve the fish stock in the sauce and cook on a high heat for two minutes, until the oil rises to the surface. Return the cauliflower, fold it into the sauce and reduce the heat to low. Cook, uncovered, for 15 minutes at a gentle simmer. Return the fish to the pan and carefully cook through for two to three minutes. Check for seasoning, then garnish with the coriander and serve.

Vegetables

Aubergine with nigella seeds

Saumya Singh, London

Serves 4

For those who expect Indian food to be made with dozens of spices, here is a an unctuous dish prepared with only one. Indians are magicians with spices. The number used is immaterial. Here, aubergine is cooked with just nigella seeds. As it browns, it picks up such a beautifully caramelised flavour that it is hard to stop eating. Also useful to know: cooking time is just six or seven minutes. Saumya, a banker, has many quick dishes at her command.

I ate it with a biryani and a raita and it was perfect. It may easily be served at Western meals, pairing comfortably with lamb chops, a roast duck, or grilled fish.

1 large aubergine (or 2 smaller), total weight 520g (1lb 3oz)
4 tablespoons olive or sunflower oil
½ teaspoon nigella seeds (kalonji)
½ teaspoon salt, or to taste

Cut the aubergine(s) into 1 centimetre (½ inch) cubes.

Pour the oil into a karhai, wok, or 25 centimetre (10 inch) frying pan over a medium-high heat. When it's really hot put in the nigella seeds and, a second later, the aubergine. Stir once or twice and sprinkle the salt over the top. Keep stirring for six or seven minutes, until the aubergine has browned lightly and is deliciously tender, then serve.

Madhur's hot and sour aubergine

Serves 4

1 large aubergine (or 2 smaller), total weight 520g (1lb 3oz)
4 tablespoons olive or sunflower oil
½ teaspoon nigella seeds (kalonji)
¼ teaspoon fennel seeds
½ teaspoon salt, or to taste
¼ teaspoon chilli powder
1½ teaspoons lemon juice
1½ teaspoons caster sugar

Here is my variation of the preceding recipe with a slight sweet and sour flavour.

Follow the recipe above up to the point when you add the nigella seeds, then, a second later, add the fennel seeds. Add the aubergine after two seconds. Stir once or twice and sprinkle the salt over the top.

Now keep cooking and stirring over a medium-high heat until the aubergine has browned lightly and is tender, about six or seven minutes. Add the chilli powder, lemon juice and sugar. Toss, then serve.

Fire-roasted aubergines with garlic and tomatoes (bharta version I)

Chaat House, Leicester

Serves 4

Indians eat aubergines with great gusto; it is a vegetable that they have known since ancient times. In India, aubergines are often roasted in tandoor ovens in states such as Punjab, or over a fire, or in hot ashes. In Britain, most people do the roasting over a gas flame or under a grill. (See page 219 for the method.) Serve this bharta with any Indian breads and with meats and vegetables of your choice.

400g can tomatoes

4 tablespoons olive or sunflower oil

2 teaspoons finely chopped garlic

15 fresh curry leaves

875g (scant 2lb) aubergines (about 3 medium), roasted, peeled and the flesh roughly chopped (see page 219)

1 teaspoon salt

1 teaspoon finely chopped hot green chilli

2 tablespoons coarsely chopped coriander leaves

Tip the can of tomatoes into a blender. Process to a purée.

Put the oil in a medium-sized pan, about 20 centimetres (8 inches) in diameter, and set it over a medium-high heat. When it's hot, put in the garlic and swirl for a second. Add the curry leaves and swirl for another three seconds. Now add the tomatoes and stir for about two minutes.

Add the aubergine flesh, mix, then tip in the salt and green chilli. Continue to stir and cook over a medium-high heat for at least five or six minutes, or until the sauce thickens. Serve garnished with the coriander.

Fire-roasted aubergines with curry leaves (bharta version II)

Shayona Restaurant, London

Serves 4

As this recipe comes from the restaurant attached to the Swaminarayan Temple, it follows all the culinary teachings of that temple. No garlic or onions are used and all the cooking is done in ghee (clarified butter).

This is much spicier and more highly seasoned than the previous recipe, and at the temple the aubergine is roasted in a hot tandoor oven. (For roasting aubergines at home, see page 219.) Serve this with Indian breads, vegetables and dals.

5 tablespoons ghee, olive or sunflower oil
½ teaspoon mustard seeds
½ teaspoon cumin seeds
5 centimetre (2 inch) cassia bark or cinnamon stick
2 cassia leaves, or bay leaves
6 fresh curry leaves
2 hot dried chillies
1 medium tomato, roughly chopped
1 tablespoon peeled, finely grated root ginger
1 tablespoon hot green chilli, finely chopped, or to taste
800g (1lb 12oz) aubergines (about 2 large), roasted,
 peeled and the flesh roughly chopped (see page 219)

½ teaspoon turmeric
½ teaspoon chilli powder
½ teaspoon salt
1 tablespoon lemon juice
2 tablespoons yogurt

For the garnish
a little ghee, olive or vegetable oil
6 or so fresh curry leaves
2 dried red chillies
1 centimetre (½ inch) peeled root ginger,
 cut into slivers

Pour the ghee or oil into a medium-sized pan about 20 centimetres (8 inches) in diameter and set over a high heat. Moving quickly, add the mustard and cumin seeds and swirl in the oil for about 15 seconds. Keep the pan moving and add the cassia bark, cassia leaves, curry leaves and dried chillies. After another 15 seconds, tip in the tomato, ginger and green chilli, stirring for two minutes until soft. Now add the aubergine flesh, turmeric, chilli powder and salt, cooking for a further two minutes. Reduce the heat to medium and add the lemon juice and yogurt. Cook for three to four minutes, stirring, then transfer to a warmed serving bowl.

Meanwhile, heat the ghee or oil for the garnish in a frying pan over a medium-high heat. When hot, throw in the curry leaves and stir for about 10 seconds, until crisp. Remove with a slotted spoon and drain on kitchen paper. Now add the chillies to the hot oil and fry, stirring, for about 30 seconds, or until they darken. Scoop them out, too, and drain on kitchen paper.

Garnish the bharta with the fried curry leaves and chillies, and the slivered ginger, then serve.

Stuffed aubergines (vengan na raviaya)

Gujarati Rasoi, London

Serves 4

This marvellous establishment, Gujarati Rasoi, sells its superbly prepared and very fresh, unadulterated, Surat-style Gujarati vegetarian foods at Borough and Broadway Markets. There is no one else like them in all of Britain. Here is their stuffed aubergine dish. Indians love to stuff small aubergines and there are probably as many recipes for them as there are communities in India. Here, mother and son team Lalita and Urvesh use peanuts in the stuffing. Serve with rice or chapatis and dal, possibly their Aduki Bean Curry (see page 126).

For the stuffing
50g (1¾oz) skinless roasted
    peanuts
60g (2oz) finely chopped
    onion
2 tablespoons peeled, finely
    grated root ginger
1½ teaspoons finely chopped
    hot green chilli
2 tablespoons crushed garlic
3 tablespoons ground
    coriander
1 tablespoon ground cumin
75g (2¾oz) coriander leaves,
    finely chopped
1 tablespoon jaggery or soft
    brown sugar
2 tablespoons lemon juice
1 teaspoon salt
½ teaspoon garam masala
6 cherry tomatoes

For the aubergines
8 small aubergines, about
    8 centimetres (3 inches) long
6 tablespoons olive or
    sunflower oil
115g (4oz) frozen peas,
    defrosted

Blitz the peanuts to a coarse powder in a food processor and pour into a mixing bowl. Place all the other ingredients for the stuffing in a blender and process to a paste. Mix well into the ground nuts.

Remove the aubergine sepals, if you like, but retain the stems. Slice each aubergine lengthways, from its bulbous end, three-quarters of the way up the stem. Make two equally spaced lengthways cross cuts, again three-quarters of the way to the stem. The aubergines should be intact, but with six segments. Stuff each by forcing the paste deep into the cuts (you should have some paste left).

Set a karhai, wok or a large pan, around 25 centimetres (10 inches) in diameter, over a medium heat. Pour in the oil and, when hot, arrange the aubergines in it, covering them all with the excess paste. Add about 2 tablespoons of water. Place the lid firmly on and cook for about 20 minutes, or until soft, uncovering every four or five minutes to carefully turn the aubergines, adding a tablespoon of water if they are sticking. Remove from the heat and sprinkle the peas on top. Cover for two minutes, or until the peas are cooked through in the rising steam. Serve hot.

Cauliflower with potatoes (aloo gobi)

Gurbax Kaur, Bradford

Serves 6

This is a Punjabi classic and, needless to say, there are many ways of cooking it. While we were filming the cookery series that accompanies this book, we spent a great deal of time searching for our ideal aloo gobi. There were many opinions. We tasted this, we tasted that. In the end, we all agreed that the perfect dish was produced by the mother of one of our own crew members. So, for me at any rate, this will always be Harjit's mum's aloo gobi. Gurbax uses all the leaf bottoms and stem sections that come with the cauliflower head. She just chops them up coarsely and cooks them with the spice mixture.

This is generally eaten with Indian breads, dal and yogurt raita.

For the deep-frying stage
sunflower oil, to deep-fry
600g (1lb 4oz) cauliflower florets, plus about 150g (5½oz) stalks and leaves, chopped
450g (1lb) potato, peeled and roughly chopped

For the rest
2 tablespoons olive or sunflower oil
1 medium onion, finely chopped

½ teaspoon cumin seeds
1 tablespoon finely grated or crushed garlic
1 tablespoon peeled, finely grated root ginger
1 medium tomato, finely chopped
3–4 hot green chillies, finely chopped
1¼ teaspoons salt
1 tablespoon dried fenugreek leaves
¾ teaspoon turmeric
2 tablespoons chopped coriander leaves

Start with the deep-frying. Pour the oil into a karhai or wok and set it over a medium-high heat. Wait for it to get very hot. Fry the cauliflower florets (not the stalks or leaves) in two batches, for about two minutes each batch, or until light brown all over. Remove and drain on kitchen paper. Ensure the oil has time to reheat between batches. Now carefully add the potato to the oil, standing back in case of splashes, and fry for five to six minutes, or until golden all over. Remove and drain on kitchen paper. (Strain the oil and save it for future use.)

Now for the rest. Set a clean karhai, wok or heavy-based pan, about 20 centimetres (8 inches) in diameter, over a medium heat. Pour in the oil and, when hot, add the onion. Sauté for two minutes, then add the cumin seeds. Stir for three to five minutes, or until the onion is light brown. Spoon in the garlic and ginger. Stir for two minutes, adding a splash of hot water if it starts to stick. Add the tomato and cook for five minutes, or until completely integrated. Sprinkle in the chillies and salt and stir for one minute. Crumble in the fenugreek, stirring for one minute. Spoon in the turmeric and mix well. Add another splash of water if necessary, then tip in the cauliflower stalks and leaves and cook, stirring, for six minutes, or until soft. Add a little water if the pan seems to dry out. Now put in the deep-fried cauliflower florets and potato and the chopped coriander, mix gently and cook for a final two minutes, then serve.

Ground greens in the Punjabi style (sarson ka saag)

Rajbiar Aulakh, London

Serves 4

In the Punjab, winter is the season when the fields are yellow with mustard flowers. This is when they cook the mustard greens and devour them with a bread made from dried corn.

Big knobs of freshly made white butter go on both. The greens are cooked in large pots, or in pressure cookers. Almost everybody in India owns at least one pressure cooker. It hastens the cooking process and saves energy. Mustard leaves are generally found only in Asian stores. If you cannot get them, you can use a combination of spring greens and spinach. If you cannot find fenugreek leaves, which give a hint of bitterness, buy dried fenugreek leaves and put in a small handful instead.

Indian grocers sell a flour made out of dried corn called 'makki atta'. If you cannot find it, use fine polenta.

450g (1lb) mustard leaves, washed and finely chopped
½ teaspoon salt
250g (9oz) spinach, washed and finely chopped
30g (1oz) fenugreek leaves, washed and finely chopped
30g (1oz) coriander leaves, washed and finely chopped
2 tablespoons dried corn flour or fine polenta (see recipe introduction)
3 tablespoons unsalted butter
1 teaspoon finely grated or crushed garlic
1 teaspoon peeled, finely grated root ginger
1 dried chilli
1 hot green chilli, finely chopped
1 medium onion, finely chopped
1 medium tomato, chopped

Set a pressure cooker over a high heat and mix in the mustard leaves and salt with 240ml (9fl oz) of water, then seal the lid and heat to full pressure. Remove from the heat and allow the pressure to drop by itself.

Open the lid and stir in the spinach, fenugreek and coriander leaves. Set over the heat again, seal the lid and heat to full pressure, then reduce the heat to its lowest setting and cook for 30 minutes. Remove from the heat and allow the pressure to drop once more.

Remove the lid and set the pan over a low heat, to remove excess moisture. Using a potato masher, pulp the greens to create a coarse mixture; you do not want a fine purée. Now add the dried corn flour or polenta slowly, stirring to avoid any lumps.

Melt the butter in a small pan over a medium heat. Add the garlic and ginger. Stir and fry for 30 seconds, then add the dried chilli, green chilli and onion. Stir and fry until the onion is soft and brown. Mix in the tomato and cook until soft. Pour the contents of this pan into the greens and mix well, then serve.

Sweet mango curry

Naina Parmar, Leicester

Serves 4

When I was on Sabras Radio in Leicester, several listeners called in offering their thoughts on Indian foods being cooked in the United Kingdom. Naina called in with this delicious recipe for a mango curry made with the Alphonso mangoes that are flown in from India during April and May. They are sold by Indian grocers and are deeply aromatic, but you can use any sweet mango that you can find. I used four Alphonso mangoes, each weighing about 200g (7oz). Once the stones were removed, I had about 500g (1lb 2oz) of flesh with skin.

Serve this curry with Tangy Rice Pancakes (see page 162), or plain rice.

4 Alphonso mangoes, or any other sweet, non-fibrous mangoes
4 tablespoons olive or sunflower oil
1 teaspoon cumin seeds
1 large onion, finely chopped
1 teaspoon finely chopped hot green chilli
2 teaspoons peeled, finely chopped root ginger
½ teaspoon turmeric
½ teaspoon salt
400g can plum tomatoes, finely chopped, with juice
¼ teaspoon garam masala (ideally Naina's Garam Masala, see page 215)
6 tablespoons finely chopped coriander leaves

Wash the mangoes well. Remove each mango stone: first, slice across the base, where it was attached to the stem. This will reveal the outline of the stone inside. Stand the mango upright and slice down each side of the stone, removing two 'cheeks' of mango flesh. Cut these into four equal strips (leave the skin on). Stand the stone upright again and carefully cut along its edges to remove the remaining flesh from there. Repeat for all the mangoes.

Set a karhai, wok or large pan, around 25 centimetres (10 inches) in diameter, over a medium heat and add the oil. When it's hot, add the cumin seeds. Let them sizzle for 10 seconds, then tip in the onion, stirring and frying for five minutes until it turns light brown. Add the chilli and ginger and mix well for one minute. Stir in the turmeric and salt and fry for one minute more.

Now pour in the tomatoes, stir and add the garam masala. Cook for 15 minutes, stirring occasionally, before sprinkling in the coriander. Reduce the heat to low, stir and simmer for three minutes, then add the mango slices. Mix thoroughly to ensure they are well coated in the sauce and continue cooking for two more minutes, then serve.

Dry okra (sookhi bhindi)

Saumya Singh, London

Serves 4

Here the okra is cooked very dry, with no sauce at all. Serve it with a dal and meat dish of your choice, with flatbread or rice. Do not wash the okra, just wipe it with a damp cloth and leave to air-dry before cutting and cooking. If you cannot get amchoor – tangy green mango powder – sprinkle 2 teaspoons of lemon juice over the top and toss just before serving.

3 tablespoons olive or sunflower oil
1 medium onion, chopped
450g (1lb) okra, topped, tailed and cut into 1 centimetre (½ inch) pieces
1 tablespoon ground coriander
1 teaspoon garam masala
½ teaspoon amchoor (green mango powder, or see recipe introduction)
¼–½ teaspoon chilli powder
½ teaspoon turmeric
¾ tsp salt

Pour the oil into a 20–25 centimetre (8–10 inch) frying pan and set it over a medium-high heat. When it's hot, tip in the onion. Stir and fry for a minute. Add the okra. Stir and fry, still over a medium-high heat, for five minutes. Now reduce the heat to medium-low and stir and fry for 10 minutes.

Reduce the heat to low. Add the ground spices and salt. Stir and cook over a low heat for five to six minutes, or until the okra is tender, then serve.

Kale cooked in an East African style (sukuma wiki)

Bimal Parmar, Coventry

Serves 2–3

In its original form, this recipe requires an East African dried wild spinach, which is hard for most people to find. It has a very chewy texture, popular in this part of Africa. We were told by Bimal, an East African Gujarati chef, that kale makes a worthy substitute, so that is what we have used here.

salt, to taste
200g (7oz) kale, rinsed and roughly chopped
3 tablespoons olive or sunflower oil
3 tablespoons finely chopped red onion
1 teaspoon grated or very finely chopped garlic
1½ teaspoons peeled, finely grated root ginger
½ teaspoon finely chopped hot green chilli
¼ teaspoon turmeric
¼ teaspoon chilli powder
1 teaspoon lemon juice
1 medium tomato, finely chopped
1 tablespoon coriander leaves, to serve

Pour 200ml (7fl oz) of water into a pan about 25 centimetres (10 inches) in diameter and bring to a boil. Add ¼ teaspoon of salt and the kale. Return to a boil. Cover, reduce the heat to low and cook for about eight minutes, or until the kale is soft (older kale will take a little longer to cook). Lift out the kale with a slotted spoon and chop finely, reserving the cooking liquid.

Put the oil into a medium-sized pan, about 20 centimetres (8 inches) in diameter, and set it over a medium heat. When it's hot, tip in the onion. Stir and fry for about five minutes, or until the pieces start to turn brown at the edges. Stir in the garlic, ginger and green chilli and fry for a further two minutes.

Now mix in the kale and add the turmeric, chilli powder, lemon juice, tomato and ¼ teaspoon more salt. Stir for two minutes, then pour in the reserved vegetable cooking liquid. Continue stirring for two minutes, allowing the tomatoes to soften and the sauce to thicken. Check the salt, then transfer to a warmed serving dish and sprinkle with the coriander leaves.

Pakora, pea and potato sabzi

Southall Gurdwara, London

Serves 8

Sikh Gurdwaras – houses of worship – serve only vegetarian meals. They need to be as nutritious as possible, so many recipes contain dried beans or bean flours. Here a kind of gnocchi made from chickpea flour, called pakoras as they belong to the general family of fried fritters and dumplings, are added to the peas and potatoes to provide extra food value. At the Gurdwara, the dough is extruded from a machine into hot oil and fried, though at home it's far easier to make it into a pasta. A sabzi is simply a vegetable dish in northern India.

For the pakoras
100g (3½oz) chickpea (gram) flour,
  plus more to dust
¼ teaspoon salt
olive or sunflower oil, to deep-fry

For the sabzi
4 tablespoons olive or sunflower oil
1 teaspoon cumin seeds

1 large onion, roughly chopped
2.5 centimetres (1 inch) peeled root ginger, in slivers
1½ teaspoons finely chopped hot green chilli
700g (1lb 9oz) potatoes, peeled and
  roughly chopped
1 teaspoon salt
200g (7oz) peas, fresh or frozen
1½ teaspoons garam masala (ideally Gurdwara's
  Special Garam Masala, see page 215)

First, make the pakoras. Place the flour and salt in a large bowl and slowly add 3½ tablespoons of water. Knead together to make a soft, pliable dough ball. Place it on a work surface dusted with flour and roll out to a sheet 0.5 centimetres (¼ inch) thick. Cut the dough with a sharp knife, making vertical lines 2.5 centimetres (1 inch) apart. Now cut parallel lines 2.5 centimetres (1 inch) apart at an angle to create diamonds. Carefully arrange them on a plate, making sure they are dusted with flour to keep them from sticking together.

Pour 2.5 centimetres (1 inch) of oil into a karhai, wok or large pan and set it over a medium-low heat. Check to see if the oil is ready by dropping in a ball of dough: it should sizzle immediately. Place in six to eight pakoras and fry for three to four minutes, turning every 45 seconds until golden, then remove and drain on kitchen paper. Make all the pakoras this way.

For the sabzi, pour the oil into a 25 centimetre (10 inch) pan and set it over a medium heat. When it is hot, add the cumin seeds and stir for 20 seconds. Add the onion, stirring and frying for five minutes until light brown at the edges. Now tip in the ginger and chilli, stir for two minutes, then add the potatoes and stir for two minutes. Add 750ml (1½ pints) of water, or enough to cover the potatoes, with the salt. Bring to a boil, cover and reduce the heat to low. Simmer for 15 minutes. Add the peas and pakoras, stir, cover and cook for five minutes, then add the garam masala. Mix well, uncover and cook for a final five minutes, then serve.

Potatoes with fresh fenugreek (butteta ne methi)

Gujarati Rasoi, London

Serves 4–6

Indians cook potatoes with anything and everything. At the Gujarati Rasoi stall at Broadway Market, they are cooked beautifully with fresh fenugreek greens. These leaves have a strong odour that stays in the pores, rather like asparagus. The greens are only sold by Indian grocers; you have to ask for fresh methi. If you cannot find them, use baby spinach and crumble in about 2 tablespoons of dried fenugreek leaves as well for the aroma. (These are sold in all Indian grocers as kasuri methi.)

*4 tablespoons olive or
   sunflower oil*
1 dried chilli
1 teaspoon mustard seeds
½ teaspoon cumin seeds
4 tablespoons coriander leaves
*1 teaspoon finely chopped hot
   green chilli*
*2 teaspoons peeled, finely
   grated root ginger*
3 teaspoons ground coriander
1 teaspoon ground cumin
½ teaspoon salt
¼ teaspoon turmeric
*600g (1lb 4oz) potatoes,
   roughly chopped*
*100g (3½oz) fresh fenugreek
   leaves, removed from stems
   and chopped*

Pour the oil into a non-stick karhai, wok or large pan about 25 centimetres (10 inches) in diameter and set it over a medium-high heat. When it's hot, drop in the dried chilli and cook until brown all over, about 20 seconds. Working quickly, add the mustard seeds. Let them pop, then add the cumin seeds, letting them sizzle. Swirl the oil to infuse, then add the coriander leaves (take care, as the oil will spit).

Reduce the heat to medium and add the green chilli and ginger, stirring and frying. Add the ground coriander and cumin, salt and turmeric, mixing well. After one minute, add the potato pieces and incorporate thoroughly into the hot spice paste.

Cook, uncovered, for to 20–25 minutes, stirring now and then, until the potatoes are tender. Gently fold in the fenugreek, cover, and remove from the heat. Allow the leaves to cook in the residual heat for a minute, then serve.

Potato and spinach curry

Yesmien Bagh Ali, Skipton, Yorkshire

Serves 4

Yesmien works for a wonderfully worthy project that brings inner-city kids from Bradford and Leeds together with often all-white kids from the Yorkshire Dales. They cook and do drama projects together, all the while living in bunk barns surrounded by the Dales, stone walls and sheep. They cook all manner of foods, from shepherd's pie to hot curries and kebabs.

This is one of the dishes her students make. I watched them do it, little blonde Maisy and dark-haired Raisa, cutting leaves of spinach side by side.

*5 tablespoons olive or
   sunflower oil*
2 medium onions, finely sliced
*6 garlic cloves, finely grated
   or crushed*
*1 tablespoon peeled, finely
   grated root ginger*
*2 medium tomatoes, roughly
   chopped*
*1½ teaspoons basaar mix
   or Kashmiri mix (ideally
   Yesmien's Basaar Mix,
   see page 216)*
½ teaspoon salt
*1 hot green chilli, finely
   chopped*
*400g (14oz, about 2 medium)
   potatoes, finely chopped*
*25g (scant 1oz) coriander
   leaves and stems, finely
   chopped*
*350g (12oz) spinach leaves,
   finely chopped*
*1 teaspoon garam masala
   (ideally Yesmien's Garam
   Masala, see page 215)*

Pour the oil into a non-stick karhai, wok or large pan, around 25 centimetres (10 inches) in diameter, and set it over a medium heat. When it's hot, add the onions. Stir and fry for about five minutes, or until soft. Mix in the garlic and ginger and continue stirring and frying for five to seven minutes, or until golden. Add the tomatoes, cover and cook for five minutes, until soft. Add the basaar mix and salt and fry for a further five minutes, until you have a deep red paste. Add the chilli and fry for one minute more.

Now mix in the potatoes and cook for five to six minutes, or until they are somewhat translucent. Add 120ml (4fl oz) of water and the chopped coriander. Mix thoroughly.

Fold in the spinach and cook, stirring, for two to three minutes. Reduce the heat to low, cover and cook for 15 minutes. Add the garam masala and stir gently to mix. Cover and cook until the potatoes are tender, then serve.

Roasted masala potatoes

Serves 4

These are designed to go with the Whole Roasted Masala Chicken (see page 82), but may be served with any roasted or grilled meats.

6 tablespoons olive or
    sunflower oil
5 medium potatoes, peeled,
    halved lengthways, and cut
    into roughly 5x4 centimetre
    (2x1½ inch) chunks
¾ teaspoon salt
¾ teaspoon freshly coarse-
    ground black pepper
1 teaspoon ground coriander
1 teaspoon ground cumin
½ teaspoon turmeric
1 teaspoon Kashmiri (mild)
    chilli powder

Preheat the oven to 180°C/350°F/gas mark 4.

Pour the oil into a large bowl. Add the potatoes and sprinkle in the salt and pepper. Ensure the potatoes are well coated, then transfer to a baking tray in a single layer. Place it in the middle of the oven and roast for 20 minutes.

Spoon the coriander, cumin, turmeric and chilli powder on to a plate and mix well. Remove the potatoes from the oven. Using tongs, roll the potatoes in the spice mix, making sure all sides are covered. Return them to the oven for a further 20 minutes, or until lightly browned and tender all the way through when pierced with a knife.

Potato and long bean curry

Chaat House, Leicester

Serves 4

Mrs Gupta often cooks this simple, very mild dish in her Leicester restaurant. I ate it first when I was filming in the town, a film that was written and directed by her son, Amit Gupta. It made me feel that I was in my own home. She served it to us cast members with chapatis, a yogurt raita and her lovely Black Dal (see page 130). Nothing could have been nicer.

Long beans, or yard long beans, are about one foot in length and are commonly found in Asian markets. If you cannot get them, use ordinary green beans instead.

5 tablespoons olive or sunflower oil
¾ teaspoon cumin seeds
1 large onion, finely chopped
1 teaspoon turmeric
500g (1lb 2oz) potatoes, cut into 2.5 centimetre (1 inch) pieces
250g (9oz) long beans, or green beans, cut into 2.5 centimetre (1 inch) lengths
salt, to taste
¾ teaspoon garam masala (ideally Chaat House's Special Garam Masala, see page 215)

Pour the oil into a medium-sized pan, about 20 centimetres (8 inches) in diameter, and set it over a medium heat. When it's hot, add the cumin seeds and cook for 15 seconds. Quickly add the onion. Stir and fry for about five minutes, or until the onion is lightly browned.

Now add the turmeric, stir once and add the potatoes, beans and salt. Mix well, cover, reduce the heat to low and cook for 15 minutes, or until the potatoes are almost done. Stir a few times during this period.

Mix in the garam masala, replace the lid and continue cooking until the potatoes are soft, about five minutes more, then serve.

Peas with fresh Indian cheese (matar paneer)

Gurbax Kaur, Bradford

Serves 4–6

Much loved by both vegetarians and non-vegetarians, the main ingredient of this dish is paneer, or fresh Indian cheese. When I first came to Britain, paneer had to be made at home, but nowadays all South Asian grocers sell it, making the dish quick and easy to prepare.

Gurbax's sauce is a particularly smooth one as she uses a stick blender during the cooking process.

This dish may be served with rice or flatbreads such as chapatis.

olive or sunflower oil, to deep-fry, plus 3 tablespoons (the deep-frying oil may be re-used)

400g (14oz) paneer, cut into 2cm (¾ inch) chunks

1 medium onion, finely chopped

1 teaspoon cumin seeds

1 teaspoon finely grated or crushed garlic

1 teaspoon peeled, finely grated root ginger

4–5 hot green chillies, finely sliced

1 teaspoon tomato purée

1¼ teaspoons salt

1 teaspoon garam masala

1 teaspoon turmeric

1 teaspoon dried fenugreek leaves (kasuri methi)

250g (9oz) frozen peas

2 tablespoons coriander leaves, to garnish

Set a karhai, wok or sturdy, deep pan for deep-frying over a medium heat and pour in the oil to deep-fry. When it's hot, add the paneer in batches. Move the chunks around with a slotted spoon to make sure they do not stick together. Fry until they are reddish-gold all over. Remove with a slotted spoon and drain on kitchen paper.

Set a medium-sized pan, about 20 centimetres (8 inches) in diameter, over a medium heat. Pour in the 3 tablespoons of oil. When it's hot, add the onion. Stir and fry for about five minutes, until it starts to turn translucent. Add the cumin seeds and continue to cook for two minutes. Add the garlic, ginger and chillies. Stir and reduce the heat, mixing well for five minutes. Add a splash of boiling water if the ingredients stick. Spoon in the tomato purée, stir, then add the salt. Stir, then remove from the heat.

Blend to a fine paste with a stick blender. (If you do not have one, cool, use a regular blender, then pour back into the pan and reheat.) Return to a medium heat. Add the garam masala, turmeric and fenugreek leaves and stir for two minutes, combining them into the paste. Add the peas, folding them into the paste, and cook for two minutes. Pour in 300ml (½ pint) of cool water. Bring to a boil, then reduce the heat to a simmer for four minutes. Tip in the paneer chunks and stir them into the sauce. Cook for a further two minutes, then garnish with the coriander to serve.

Dals

Aduki bean curry

Gujarati Rasoi, London

Serves 4–6

This is a very fine curry that I first ate at the Gujarati Rasoi stall in Borough Market, London. It was served with a rice dish made with cumin seeds. You could try it with Cashew Nut and Curry Leaf Rice (see page 146). You will have to start the night before, to soak the beans.

200g (7oz) aduki beans
2 tablespoons brown sugar
5 tablespoons olive or
    sunflower oil
½ teaspoon mustard seeds
3 centimetre (generous 1 inch)
    cassia bark or
    cinnamon stick
1 dried chilli
1 garlic clove, roughly sliced,
    plus 1 teaspoon finely
    chopped garlic
2 teaspoons peeled, finely
    grated root ginger
2 hot green chillies, finely
    sliced
2 teaspoons ground coriander
½ teaspoon ground cumin
½ teaspoon turmeric
1 teaspoon salt
1 teaspoon garam masala
60g (2oz) finely chopped
    onion
125g (4½oz) tomato passata
15g (½oz) coriander leaves,
    chopped
6 tablespoons grated fresh
    coconut, or frozen grated
    coconut, defrosted
3 tablespoons lemon juice

Rinse the beans well and soak them overnight in 1.5 litres (2¾ pints) of water in a pan about 20 centimetres (8 inches) in diameter.

Next day, set the pan over a high heat, add the sugar and bring to a boil. Reduce the heat to low, cover partially and cook for an hour and a half, or until the beans are very soft and broken up. Pour into a large bowl and set aside.

Clean the pan and place it over a medium heat. Pour in the oil. Check it is hot by dropping in a few of the mustard seeds; they should sizzle and pop immediately. Working quickly, add the cassia bark, followed almost immediately by the dried chilli. Allow this to darken all over for 20 seconds, then add the remaining mustard seeds and let them pop for a few seconds. Add the sliced garlic, swirl the pan and then add, all at the same time, the ginger, green chillies, ground coriander and cumin, turmeric, salt and garam masala. This process should take about one minute. Stir for a further minute, then add the onion and the finely chopped garlic. Reduce the heat to medium-low and stir and fry for two minutes, or until the onions are soft.

Add the passata and cook, stirring, for three minutes. Return the beans and their cooking liquid, bring to a gentle simmer and cook, uncovered, for a further 10–15 minutes. Add water if it's too thick, to achieve a consistency you like.

Add the chopped coriander, coconut and lemon juice. Give the dish one final stir, then serve.

Mixed black dal

Southall Gurdwara, London

Serves 8

In Southall, West London, is the largest gurdwara, or Sikh temple, outside India. Its golden dome beckons thousands of worshippers, who come from miles around. It did not even exist when I first came to Britain. Now, there are 200 such houses of worship in the UK, offering spiritual nourishment to the growing number of Sikhs in the country.

The gurdwara, like all such temples the world over, also offers another kind of nourishment – food – to those who are hungry. No one is turned away. Its langar, or food hall, serves 1,500 people a day, and 2,500 at weekends. Preparations start at 1am. The food is prepared by the faithful, who offer their services free. They cook in a vast, modern, spotlessly clean kitchen. Certain strictures apply: the food must be simple, fresh and nourishing, with not too much salt, sugar, spices or oil; it must be vegetarian; no garlic may be used; and the langar must express the ideals of sharing, inclusiveness and the oneness of all mankind. All the money for the food is donated.

We watched several dozen women with their heads covered standing on both sides of long, steel tables, rolling out and cooking hundreds of chapatis. It was a beautiful sight.

This dish is made with whole and split legumes. If you cannot get one of the varieties, substitute that amount with more of the others. The slow cooking makes the dish delicious and digestible. You'll need to soak the beans the night before. Serve with chapatis or naan.

100g (3½oz) whole urad dal
    with skin
100g (3½oz) whole mung dal
    with skin
100g (3½oz) chana dal
100g (3½oz) moth beans
2 medium onions, finely
    chopped
2 centimetres (¾ inch) peeled
    root ginger, cut into slivers
3 teaspoons finely chopped hot
    green chilli
60g (2oz) unsalted butter
1¾ teaspoons salt
½ teaspoon turmeric
4 teaspoons garam masala
    (ideally Gurdwara's Garam
    Masala, see page 215)

The night before, pick over all four types of dal and rinse them all well. Combine all the dals in a large, heavy-based pan about 25 centimetres (10 inches) in diameter. Pour in 2 litres (3½ pints) of water and leave to soak overnight.

Next day, place the pan over a high heat and add the onions, ginger, chilli, butter, salt and turmeric. Cover and bring to a boil, then reduce the heat to low and simmer at a gentle bubble for about two and a half hours, stirring occasionally.

Check for seasoning, then add the garam masala, mix thoroughly, cover and continue cooking for 15 minutes, then serve.

Black dal

~~~~~~

Chaat House, Leicester

Serves 3

Here the dal used is urad, a black-skinned dal that is split but not hulled. Ask for urad dal with skin. One side will look black, the other white. It is cooked very simply here to make a healthy, nourishing dish. Serve with rice or Indian flatbreads – such as chapatis – and a vegetable dish, plus a yogurt raita.

100g (3½oz) split urad dal with skins
½ medium onion, sliced
¼ teaspoon turmeric
¼ teaspoon salt, plus more to taste
4 teaspoons tomato purée
2 teaspoons olive or sunflower oil
¼ teaspoon ground asafoetida
1 teaspoon cumin seeds
1 hot green chilli, finely sliced
1 centimetre (½ inch) peeled root ginger, very finely chopped

Rinse the dal, then soak it in a medium-sized pan, about 20 centimetres (8 inches) in diameter, in 500ml (18fl oz) of tepid water. Leave it for at least one hour.

Now set the pan over a medium heat and bring to a boil with the onion and turmeric. Add the salt and half the tomato purée, stir, then reduce the heat to low. Simmer, covered, for about 1½ hours, or until the dal is very soft. Uncover and add a large pinch of salt.

Set an equivalent sized pan over a medium-high heat. Pour in the oil and, when it's hot, add the asafoetida, which will immediately fizz. Swirl the pan, then add the cumin seeds. Tilt the pan to ensure the seeds are all covered by the hot oil and cook for 10 seconds, until they have browned. Reduce the heat to medium and add the chilli and ginger. Tilt again, frying for 30 seconds. Then add the remaining tomato purée and stir and fry for one minute, or until the oil separates.

Increase the heat to high for 20 seconds, until the paste bubbles, then pour it into the dal. This will bubble violently for a few seconds until the heat subsides. Turn off the heat and allow to rest for a few minutes before serving.

Chana dal cooked with mung dal

Lahore Kebab House, London

Serves 4

Here is a simple Pakistani recipe for chana dal, where the smaller-grained mung dal is used very cleverly to make a sauce. Serve with rice or flatbreads, along with a meat dish and some greens. Lemon or lime wedges may be offered on the side.

200g (7oz) chana dal
120g (4oz) skinned and split
  mung dal
1¼ teaspoons cumin seeds
¼ teaspoon turmeric
½ teaspoon chilli powder
¼ teaspoon freshly ground
  black pepper
¾ teaspoon salt
5 tablespoons olive or
  sunflower oil
1 medium onion, halved and
  finely sliced
2½ centimetres (1 inch) peeled
  root ginger, cut into slivers

Wash both dals very well, then drain. Put them, along with 1.5 litres (2¾ pints) of water, into a large, deep pan about 20 centimetres (8 inches) in diameter, and set it over a high heat. Bring to a boil. Reduce the heat to low, cover partially and cook for 50 minutes, or until the dals are tender.

Remove the lid and add the cumin seeds, turmeric, chilli powder, black pepper and salt. Stir and continue to cook, uncovered, at a gentle bubble, for another 10 minutes.

Pour the oil into a medium frying pan about 20 centimetres (8 inches) in diameter and set it over a medium heat. When it's hot, add the onion. Stir and fry for about five minutes, or until the onion turns light brown. Add the ginger and stir and fry for another minute. Pour the contents of the frying pan, including the oil, over the hot dal. Stir well and cook over a very low heat for five more minutes, before serving in warmed dishes.

Chickpeas with tomato (chhole)

Chaat House, Leicester

Serves 4

This is Sarita Udaniya's specialty. She is the sister of restaurant owner Sarla Gupta, and works with her. They are from Madhya Pradesh, so cook north Indian dishes. For spicier chickpeas, add ½ teaspoon of chilli powder with the tomato purée. This may be eaten with any flatbread and a selection of vegetables, or a yogurt raita and a simple salad.

You will need to start the day before, soaking the chickpeas overnight.

200g (7oz) dried chickpeas
½ large onion, finely chopped,
    plus 1 medium onion,
    finely sliced
2½ centimetres (1 inch) peeled
    root ginger, cut into slivers
3 tablespoons olive or
    sunflower oil
1 teaspoon cumin seeds
4 tablespoons tomato purée
½ teaspoon salt
1 teaspoon garam masala
    (ideally Chaat House's
    Special Garam Masala,
    see page 215)

The night before, wash the chickpeas well, then place in a large bowl with 1.5 litres (2¾ pints) of water.

Next day, put the chickpeas and their soaking liquid into a large, deep pot about 25 centimetres (10 inches) in diameter, along with the chopped onion and the ginger. Bring to a boil over a high heat. Cover partially, reduce the heat to low and cook slowly for one to three hours, or until the chickpeas are very tender. (Or you could use a pressure cooker. Cook on full pressure for 17 minutes, then turn off the heat and let the pressure drop by itself.) Drain the chickpeas and set aside, reserving the liquid. Add enough water to the cooking liquid to make it up to 375ml (13fl oz).

Clean out and dry the same pot. Pour in the oil and set it over a medium heat. When it's hot, add the cumin seeds and let them sizzle for 10 seconds. Add the sliced onion and stir and fry for about five minutes, or until it turns light brown. Mix in the tomato purée and stir well for two minutes. Add the salt and return the chickpeas to the pot. Mix well. Pour in the reserved chickpea liquid and bring to a simmer. Add the garam masala and simmer over a low heat, uncovered, for another 10 minutes. Serve hot.

Chickpea flour spread (pitla)

Sarojini Gulhane, London

Serves 4

A pitla is a kind of paste or spread made from the nutritious chickpea flour. It is much loved by Maharashtrians. It has been used in Bombay as a political symbol, with one Maharashtrian party promising workers not exactly a 'chicken in every pot', but enough wages to buy a pitla every day. Serve with chapatis, or spread on toast.

100g (3½oz) chickpea (gram)
*   flour*
120ml (4fl oz) yogurt
3 tablespoons olive or
*   sunflower oil*
¼ teaspoon mustard seeds
¼ teaspoon cumin seeds
12 fresh curry leaves
½ medium onion, chopped
2 teaspoons finely chopped
*   garlic*
1 tablespoon peeled, finely
*   chopped root ginger*
¼ teaspoon turmeric
½ teaspoon chilli powder
½ teaspoon salt
1 tablespoon lemon juice
30g (1oz) roughly chopped
*   coriander leaves*

Mix the chickpea flour with the yogurt and 175ml (6fl oz) of cold water and whisk it to a thick batter.

Pour the oil into a small pan, about 18 centimetres (7 inches) in diameter, and set it over a high heat. Check to see if the oil is hot enough by dropping a few mustard seeds in: they should fizz immediately. Working quickly, add the remaining mustard seeds and allow to pop. Add the cumin seeds, swirling the pan for 10 seconds. Sprinkle in the curry leaves – be careful as these will spit in the hot oil – and swirl again for 10 seconds. Add the onion, then reduce the heat to medium. Stir and fry for one minute, then mix in the garlic and ginger, stirring for one minute. Add the turmeric, chilli powder and salt. Stir for one minute.

Now pour in the chickpea batter and combine well; it will immediately start to thicken. Cook for two minutes. Pour in 80ml (3fl oz) of boiling water and mix thoroughly. Reduce the heat to low and stir for five minutes from the base of the pan, so the mixture does not catch and burn. Sprinkle the lemon juice and coriander leaves over the top.

Yogurt sauce with broad beans (kadhi)

Shayona Restaurant, London

Serves 4

Kadhis are yogurt sauces. As yogurt curdles when it is heated, Indians add small amounts of chickpea flour to stabilise it. After that, anything from seasonings, vegetables, beans and dumplings may be added to make very nutritious and delicious dishes.

This particular recipe comes from the Shayona restaurant which, in turn, is attached to the large, beautifully hand-carved Swaminarayan Temple in north-west London. I lived not too far away when I first came to London as a drama student. It did not exist then.

Here all the cooking is done in ghee, as prescribed, and garlic and onions, which are supposed to incite the baser emotions, are never used. This dish is one of Chef Ramdas Parwar's specialities.

As kadhis are fairly liquid, they are usually served with rice. When eaten with chapatis, they are served in small individual bowls.

4 teaspoons chickpea (gram) flour
500ml (18fl oz) yogurt
4 teaspoons olive or sunflower oil, or ghee
¼ teaspoon mustard seeds
¼ teaspoon cumin seeds
¼ teaspoon ground asafoetida
5 cloves
2½ centimetre (1 inch) cassia bark or cinnamon stick
1 cassia leaf or bay leaf
2 teaspoons peeled, finely chopped root ginger
1 teaspoon finely chopped hot green chilli
½ teaspoon salt
2 teaspoons caster sugar
80g (3oz) fresh or frozen broad beans, skinned and roughly chopped

Put the chickpea flour into a bowl. Slowly add a little bit of the yogurt, whisking as you go to ensure that there are no lumps. Now add the rest of the yogurt; keep whisking to get a smooth mixture. Pour in 330ml (11fl oz) of water and incorporate thoroughly.

Pour the oil into a medium-sized pan about 20 centimetres (8 inches) in diameter and set it over a medium heat. Working quickly, add the mustard and cumin seeds and the asafoetida to the hot oil and tilt the pan to ensure all the spices are covered and popping. After 15 seconds, add the cloves, cassia bark and leaf, tilting again. Then add the ginger, chilli, salt and sugar. Stir and fry for one minute, then pour in the yogurt mixture (be careful as this will bubble vigorously for a few seconds). Bring to a boil.

Reduce the heat to low and simmer for 10 minutes. Add the beans and simmer for another 10 minutes, then serve.

Red lentil and chana dal

Shafiq Rahman, Skipton, Yorkshire

Serves 6

Shafiq lives in Skipton, a town surrounded by the Yorkshire Dales. His family came from Peshawar, in north-western Pakistan. This is one of his hearty Peshawari dishes.

Shafiq likes to eat this on rice, or with hot buttery chapatis, or crusty French bread.

200g (7oz) masoor dal
100g (3½oz) chana dal
1½ teaspoons basaar mix or
    other Kashmiri spice mix
1 hot green chilli, halved
30g (1oz) coriander leaves
    and stems, finely chopped
1¼ teaspoons salt
5 tablespoons olive or
    sunflower oil
2.5 centimetres (1 inch) peeled
    root ginger, cut into slivers
4 garlic cloves, finely sliced

Pick over both types of dal, then rinse well and drain. Put them both in a pan about 25 centimetres (10 inches) in diameter. Pour in 2 litres (3½ pints) of water, the basaar mix, chilli, coriander and salt, and bring to a boil over a high heat. Reduce the heat to a simmer and cook gently for 1½ hours, stirring occasionally.

Pour the oil into a small frying pan and set it over a medium-high heat. When it's hot, add the ginger and stir and fry for 30 seconds. Now tip in the garlic and continue to stir and fry for another minute, or until light brown. Pour the contents of the frying pan, including the oil, into the hot dal and mix well. Cook for two minutes more, then serve piping hot.

Rice, breads and pancakes

Plain yellow rice

Serves 4

Here is a simple, everyday rice. The turmeric gives it a lovely yellow colour and adds its health-giving qualities of acting as an antiseptic and anti-inflammatory to the dish as well. If you wish to make plain white rice, just leave out the turmeric.

225ml (8fl oz) basmati
   rice, measured in a glass
   measuring jug
½ teaspoon turmeric
½ teaspoon salt

Wash the rice in several changes of water, until the water runs clear, then drain it. Leave it to soak in ample water for 30 minutes. Drain once more.

Meanwhile, preheat the oven to 150°C/300°F/gas mark 2.

Put the drained rice in a medium-sized, oven- and flameproof pan which has a lid, about 18 centimetres (7 inches) in diameter. Set it over a medium-high heat. Add 275ml (½ pint) of water, the turmeric and the salt. Stir to mix and bring to a boil.

Cover tightly, first with a piece of foil and then with the lid. Place in the oven and cook for 30 minutes.

Coconut rice

Claire Fisher, Ganapati Restaurant, London

Serves 4

A lovely light, aromatic dish that goes particularly well with fish, shellfish and vegetables. I love it with Goan Prawn Curry (see page 86).

1 tablespoon olive or sunflower oil
¼ teaspoon fenugreek seeds
2 garlic cloves, quartered lengthways
½ medium onion, finely sliced
12 fresh curry leaves
200g (7oz) basmati rice
250ml (9fl oz) coconut milk
¼ teaspoon salt

Set a small, heavy-based pan, about 18 centimetres (7 inches) in diameter, over a medium heat (the pan should have a lid). Pour in the oil and, when it's hot, add the fenugreek seeds. Stir for five seconds and allow to darken just a little before adding the garlic, onion and curry leaves. Stir for four to five minutes until the onion softens and starts to brown at the edges.

Mix in the rice, then add the coconut milk, 250ml (9fl oz) of water, and the salt. Stir gently and bring to a boil.

Now cover tightly and cook on the lowest heat possible for 15 minutes. Then remove from the heat and let the pan sit, undisturbed, for 10 minutes. Finally, uncover, fluff through with a fork, and serve.

Rice with peas (matar pullao)

Rubina Haider, London

Serves 6

This simple pullao gets its rich brown colour from the seasonings used in the stock. In much of Pakistan it is eaten with a raita (see Rubina's Cucumber, Onion and Mint Raita, page 193). You may also serve it with meat, chicken or fish curries.

400g (14oz) basmati rice
4 tablespoons olive or
   sunflower oil
2 medium onions, finely
   sliced
4 garlic cloves, finely sliced
½ teaspoon black
   peppercorns
½ teaspoon cumin seeds
½ teaspoon cloves
½ teaspoon coriander seeds
5 black cardamom pods
15 centimetre (6 inch)
   cassia bark or cinnamon
   stick, broken up
5 cassia leaves or bay
   leaves
1½ teaspoons salt
225g (8oz) frozen peas,
   rinsed and defrosted

Rinse the rice several times, until the water runs clear, then soak it in ample water for 30 minutes. Drain.

Set a large pan, about 25 centimetres (10 inches) in diameter, over a medium-high heat (the pan should have a lid). Pour in the oil and, when it's hot, add the onions. Stir and fry for five minutes until they turn light brown. Add the garlic. Mix well for one minute, then add the peppercorns, cumin seeds, cloves, coriander seeds, cardamom pods, cassia bark and leaves.

Stir and fry for about five minutes more, until the onions are dark brown and caramelised. Pour in 1 litre (1¾ pints) of water with the salt and bring to a boil.

Add the rice to this spicy broth and boil, uncovered, for six to seven minutes, or until most of the water has evaporated. Check by parting the rice with a spoon; you should see a little water halfway down.

Drape a clean, damp tea towel over the inside of the lid of the pan. Cover the pan with your tea towel-clad lid, pulling the ends of the towel out the way of the flame and over the lid. Reduce the heat to low and cook for 10 minutes.

Uncover and sprinkle in the peas. Mix them in gently with a fork, fluffing up the rice, then cover again for a final two to three minutes. Serve.

Cashew nut and curry leaf rice

Nikita Gulhane, London

Serves 4

This is a rice that can be eaten on its own, or served with a plain dal or a chicken dish such as Chicken in a Coconut Sauce (see page 70).

200g (7oz) basmati rice
1 tablespoon olive or
*   sunflower oil*
1 teaspoon mustard seeds
1 teaspoon cumin seeds
20 fresh curry leaves, roughly
*   shredded, a few kept whole*
100g (3½oz) split raw
*   cashews*
¾–1 teaspoon salt

Rinse the rice several times until the water runs clear. Drain, then transfer the rice to a small pan, around 18 centimetres (7 inches) in diameter. Soak it in 425ml (15fl oz) of water for 30 minutes.

Set the pan over a medium heat and bring to a boil. Cover and continue to cook over the lowest heat possible for 15 minutes. Remove from the heat, but keep the pan covered for 10 minutes.

Set a medium-sized non-stick karhai, wok or large frying pan over a medium heat. Pour in the oil and, when it's hot, add the mustard seeds. Allow to pop, then add the cumin seeds and curry leaves. Stir and fry for 15 seconds. Add the cashew nuts and salt, stir, and let the nuts turn golden. Tip in the rice and mix together, ensuring that the spices and nuts are evenly distributed throughout the rice, then serve.

Rice with toor dal and vegetables (khichri version I)

Shayona Restaurant, London

Serves 8–10

Khichri, a simple, nourishing dish of rice and dal cooked together, is of ancient origin and is eaten in varying forms all across India. This version, from Shayona, the restaurant attached to the Swaminarayan Temple in London, adds vegetables to make a full meal. Only a yogurt relish is needed.

100g (3½oz) toor dal
500g (1lb 2oz) basmati rice
3 tablespoons olive or sunflower oil
1 teaspoon mustard seeds
5 cloves
4 dried hot chillies
3 x 2½ centimetre (1 inch) cassia bark or cinnamon sticks
4 cassia leaves or bay leaves
1 teaspoon cumin seeds
6 fresh curry leaves
1 teaspoon finely chopped garlic
1 teaspoon peeled, finely chopped root ginger
1 teaspoon turmeric
½ teaspoon chilli powder
1 teaspoon salt
80g (3oz) frozen peas

80g (3oz) frozen green beans
80g (3oz) carrots, finely chopped
100g (3½oz) red pepper, roughly chopped
90g (3¼oz) aubergine, roughly chopped
90g (3¼oz) cauliflower florets, halved
½ teaspoon garam masala
1 tablespoon unsalted butter
40g (1½oz) cashew nuts

For the garnish
a little olive or sunflower oil
handful of fresh curry leaves
small handful of chopped coriander leaves
a few cashew nuts (optional)
a few slices of different coloured sweet peppers (optional)

Separately rinse the dal and rice and soak in ample water, again separately, for 20 minutes, while you get on with the rest of the dish.

Pour the oil into a large, deep, heavy-based pan about 25 centimetres (10 inches) in diameter and set it over a high heat. Check it is hot enough by dropping in a few mustard seeds: they should pop immediately. Working quickly to infuse the oil, add the cloves, dried chillies, cassia bark and leaves. Stir once. Quickly add the remaining mustard seeds, the cumin seeds and curry leaves, again swirling the hot oil. Stir in the garlic and ginger and fry. Now carefully pour in 1 litre (1¾ pints) of hot water. This will cause a violent bubbling but it will subside after a few seconds.

Add the turmeric, chilli powder and salt. Bring to a boil, then add the drained dal and continue to boil for four minutes. Now add all the vegetables and the drained rice and mix well for a minute. Reduce the heat to medium, cover and cook for 10 minutes.

Uncover, add the garam masala, butter and cashew nuts, stir gently, cover again and cook for five minutes over a low heat.

Meanwhile, heat the oil for the garnish in a small frying pan over a medium-high heat. When it's hot, throw in the curry leaves and stir for about 10 seconds, until crisp. Remove with a slotted spoon and place on kitchen paper.

Garnish the khichri with the coriander leaves and fried curry leaves, adding the cashews and sweet pepper slices, if desired, then serve.

Rice and mung dal (khichri version II)

Sarojini Gulhane, London

Serves 6

Here is another khichri. In the central Indian state of Maharashtra, where Sarojini is from, the dish is most often accompanied by kadhi (see Yogurt Sauce with Broad Beans, page 136), as the addition of anything with yogurt makes it a balanced meal, with a small salad of cucumber and onion, and some hot pickle.
    This dish is perfect for children: my granddaughter has loved a similar recipe since she was eight months old.

225g (8oz) basmati rice, rinsed and drained
100g (3½oz) skinned and split mung dal, rinsed and drained
2 teaspoons olive or sunflower oil
2 cloves
¼ teaspoon turmeric
½ teaspoon salt
1 tablespoon unsalted butter

Tip the rice and mung beans together into a medium-sized pan around 20 centimetres (8 inches) in diameter. Pour in 620ml (generous 1 pint) of water and soak for 30 minutes.

Add the oil, cloves and turmeric and bring to a boil. Stir in the salt, cover and reduce the heat, simmering gently for about 13 minutes. Remove from the heat and rest the khichri for 10 minutes.

Fork in the butter and mix well to fluff up before serving.

Rice cooked with chicken in an aromatic chicken broth (yakhni pullao)

Bashan Rafique, London

Serves 4

This was my favourite pilaf, or pullao, when I was a child. It was not hot and spicy, just comforting and very aromatic with the flavours and smells of cardamom and cinnamon and fennel and cloves. It is usually served with a yogurt raita, but at our home we also had vegetable dishes on the table.

400g (14oz) basmati rice
2 teaspoons coriander seeds
2 teaspoons fennel seeds
½ teaspoon black peppercorns
6 cloves
2 black cardamom pods
1 green cardamom pod
6 boneless, skinless chicken
    thighs
1 medium onion, peeled
1 head of garlic
5 centimetre (2 inch) piece root
    ginger, unpeeled
1 teaspoon salt
4 tablespoons olive or
    sunflower oil
1 tablespoon whole milk
generous pinch of saffron
    threads
a few drops of yellow food
    colouring (optional)

Rinse the rice well and soak it in water to cover generously for 30 minutes, while you get on with the rest of the dish.

Gather the coriander and fennel seeds, the peppercorns, cloves and both types of cardamom pods and tie them into a muslin pouch. Place in a deep pan about 25 centimetres (10 inches) in diameter with the chicken, whole onion, whole head of garlic and piece of ginger.

Pour in 1 litre (1¾ pints) of water, place over a medium heat and bring to a boil. Skim off the foam as it rises. After 10 minutes, remove the chicken and reserve. Continue boiling the liquid for five minutes, skimming off any more foam to leave a clear broth. Stir in the salt, then strain and reserve the broth.

Dry the pan and set it over a medium heat. Pour in the oil and, when it's hot, add the drained rice, stirring gently but continuously for one minute. Return the chicken and sauté with the rice for two minutes. Pour in the yakhni or broth, stir well, cover and cook over a medium-low heat for about 20 minutes, until the surface rice grains are plump.

Meanwhile, pour the milk into a small pan with the saffron and bring to a boil. Reduce the heat, tilt the pan and allow the saffron to infuse the milk. Remove from the heat.

When the rice is cooked, remove the lid and pour small amounts of the saffron milk over it to give a golden mottling. Add to this with a few drops of food colouring, if you like. Stir just before serving.

Lahore lamb biryani

Saleem Zahid, London

Serves 6–8

Here is a wonderful lamb biryani that is fairly simple to prepare. As biryanis are served on special occasions, this recipe makes a somewhat larger quantity than do most in this book.

Persian prunes, which are black in colour and sweet and sour in taste, are often added to biryanis for extra flavour. They are sold in South Asian shops as Persian prunes or 'aloo Bukhara'. If you find them and wish to add them, remember that they have a hard stone, so be careful when biting into them. Kewda water is South Asia's vanilla and comes from the screwpine family; it is sold in South Asian groceries. Rose water may be used as an alternative.

Do not worry about the amount of oil. This is a rich dish, and the oil is needed to fry the spices, the ginger and garlic, the meat, and the onions. In fact, often the dish is layered with ghee or butter instead!

Usually biryanis are simply served with yogurt raitas, but feel free to add other meat and vegetable dishes to make a grand spread.

A biryani should be very gently mixed just before serving to distribute the aromas... here, of saffron, kewda water, and meat juices.

250ml (9fl oz) olive or sunflower oil
2 tablespoons ghee
3 cassia leaves or bay leaves
5 centimetre (2 inch) cassia bark or
   cinnamon stick
8–10 black peppercorns
7–8 cloves
1 black cardamom pod, lightly crushed
6–7 green cardamom pods, lightly crushed
1 teaspoon crushed garlic
1 teaspoon peeled, finely grated root ginger
450g (1lb) boneless lamb, from shoulder or
   neck or both, cut into 2.5–4 centimetre
   (1–1½ inch) pieces

3 medium onions, about 450g (1lb), chopped
500ml (18fl oz) yogurt, lightly beaten until smooth
4 hot green chillies, cut into 1 centimetre
   (½ inch) segments
handful of chopped coriander leaves
salt
2 dried aloo Bukhara Persian prunes, if available
   (see recipe introduction, optional)
450g (1lb) basmati rice
generous pinch of ground saffron
1 capful (the cap of the bottle) kewda water
   (see recipe introduction)

Recipe continued overleaf

Put the oil and ghee in a heavy-based 25 centimetre (10 inch) pan and set it over a medium-high heat. When it's hot, add the cassia leaves and bark, peppercorns, cloves, and both types of lightly crushed cardamom pods. Stir a few times, then add the garlic and ginger. Stir once or twice, then put in the meat. Stir and fry the meat for about five minutes, or until it is lightly browned.

Now add the onions. Stir and cook, still over a medium-high heat, for about five minutes, or until the onions have softened. Reduce the heat to low and stir in the yogurt. Add the green chillies, coriander leaves, 1 teaspoon of salt and the aloo Bukharas, if using. Keep stirring and bring to a vigorous simmer, reducing the heat to medium-low. Cover partially and cook, stirring now and then, for 25 minutes. Uncover, stir and cook for another 10–15 minutes, or until the sauce is very thick and paste-like and the oil separates from the meat. Set aside, covered.

Meanwhile, preheat the oven to 150°C/300°F/gas mark 2. Rinse the rice in several changes of water, then leave to soak in ample fresh water for 15–20 minutes. Drain and leave in the strainer.

Bring about 5 litres (9 pints) of water to a boil in a large pot, the kind you use for boiling pasta. When it is boiling rapidly, add 4 teaspoons of salt and stir. Set a colander in the sink.

Add the rice to the rapidly boiling water. Stir to separate the grains, cover partially and return to a boil. Boil the rice for five to six minutes, or until a grain, when pressed hard between the fingers, has only a thin hard core at the centre and breaks into two or three pieces. Drain quickly and leave in the colander.

Tilt the pot of meat and spoon out all the fat and oil into a small bowl. Pour half of this oil into a heavy-based 25 centimetre (10 inch) ovenproof pan that has a tight-fitting lid, and spread it out. Now spread half the rice over the oil. Spoon all the meat over the rice. Sprinkle the saffron over the meat. Spread the remaining rice over the meat and then the remaining oil over the top of everything. End with the kewda water, sprinkling it over the top.

Cover tightly with foil and then the lid and place in the centre of the hot oven for 30–40 minutes, or until the rice is cooked through. Mix very gently with a slotted spoon before serving.

Chicken biryani
(kachche murgh ki biryani)

Zahda Saeed, London

Serves 6

A good biryani is loved by most people in South Asia. It does require talent – a special hand, as we say – to put a great one together. However, it is one thing to make a biryani with meat that has already been cooked: you simply layer the rice and meat, then slow-cook the two together (as in the Lahore Lamb Biryani recipe, left). It is quite another thing to cook a biryani with raw, marinated meat. Your timing has to be exact, so the rice and meat cook at the same time.

Zahda Saeed, who is originally from the Punjab, makes this superb 'raw' chicken biryani. (The meat needs to be marinated overnight, so plan ahead.)

If you cannot get the egg yellow food colouring, use any other yellow colouring to get a strong saffron colour. The amount you need will vary. If you use liquid yellow food colouring, ½ teaspoon will do.

Biryanis are traditionally served with a yogurt raita and a simple salad.

For the marinade
20g (¾oz) mint leaves, finely chopped
160ml (5½fl oz) yogurt
1 teaspoon chilli powder
2 hot green chillies, roughly chopped
1 teaspoon salt, plus more to taste
1 tablespoon garam masala

For the biryani
1 medium-sized chicken, about 1.4kg (3lb 3oz), skinned and jointed into 12 pieces
125g (4½oz) slightly salted butter
3 medium onions, finely sliced into rings
3–4 hot green chillies, halved lengthways
2 x 10 centimetre (4 inch) cassia bark or cinnamon sticks, broken up
5 black cardamom pods
3 green cardamom pods
1 tablespoon cumin seeds
5 black peppercorns
300g (10½oz) basmati rice
150g (5½oz) dried aloo Bukhara Persian prunes, stone in (see page 152), or 75g (2¾oz) dried cranberries
¼ teaspoon saffron threads, soaked in 4 tablespoons of hot water
1 teaspoon egg yellow food colouring mixed with 90ml (3¼fl oz) whole milk
3 tablespoons lemon juice

Recipe continued overleaf

Place all the marinade ingredients in a blender and blend until smooth. Pour over the chicken pieces in a non-reactive bowl, turn to coat, cover and marinate overnight, or for at least three hours, in the fridge.

The next day, melt the butter in a large karhai or wok and fry the onions for five minutes. Add the halved chillies and continue to stir and fry for five more minutes, until the onions are brown. Set aside.

Bring 2.75 litres (5 pints) of water to a boil in a large, deep, heavy-based pan about 20 centimetres (10 inches) in diameter and 15 centimetres (6 inches) deep (it must have a tight-fitting lid). Drop in the cassia bark, both types of cardamom, the cumin seeds and peppercorns and boil, uncovered, for 20 minutes to infuse. Add the rice. Once it has returned to a boil, boil for about 1½ minutes, drain, and set aside with the whole spices. The grains of rice should still be brittle and not soft.

Clean and dry the pan and place the marinated chicken at the bottom. Spoon half the rice over the chicken pieces until they are just covered. Sprinkle in a pinch of salt, then layer in half the onions and some of the butter in which they were fried. Now arrange half the aloo Bukharas or cranberries over the top, and add some more of the butter. Sprinkle in a pinch of salt again, then cover with the remaining rice, then the remaining onions and prunes. Pour the saffron and water, food colouring and milk, and lemon juice over the top, distributing it evenly.

Drape a clean, damp tea towel over the inside of the lid of the pan. Cover the pan with your tea towel-clad lid, pulling the ends of the towel out the way of the flame and over the lid.

Set the pan over a medium-high heat for 10 minutes, then reduce the heat to medium-low for a further 10 minutes, then finally reduce the heat once more to very low for the last 20 minutes.

Mix the biryani very gently with a slotted spoon, and serve.

Sweet yellow rice (meetha pullao)

Serves 4

A very Muslim dish, this slightly sweet rice should be eaten with rather spicy curries as a glorious contrast. As it contains saffron and nuts, it is considered a dish fit for a banquet.

½ teaspoon saffron threads
2 tablespoons warmed
    whole milk
200g (7oz) basmati rice
3 tablespoons ghee or butter
4 green cardamom pods
2.5 centimetre (1 inch)
    cinnamon stick
¼ teaspoon liquid yellow food
    colouring
½ teaspoon salt
15g (½oz) blanched, slivered
    almonds, plus more to serve
1 tablespoon sultanas, plus
    more to serve
90g (3¼oz) caster sugar, or
    to taste
1 sheet of silver leaf (known
    as 'vark' in Indian grocers),
    to serve (optional)

Put the saffron in a small, heavy-based frying pan set over a medium heat. Stir it about until the threads turn a few shades darker. Put the milk in a cup and crumble in the saffron, then set aside for three hours.

Wash the rice in several changes of water, then drain. Leave it to soak in 1.2 litres (2 pints) of water for 30 minutes. Drain and leave in the colander for 20 minutes.

Preheat the oven to 150°C/300°F/gas mark 2.

Heat the ghee in a wide, heavy-based, flame- and ovenproof pan over a medium heat. When it's hot, put in the cardamom and cinnamon and stir them about for a second. Now put in the rice. Stir and sauté the rice gently for about three minutes, reducing the heat slightly if it begins to catch. Add 325ml (11fl oz) of water, the food colouring and the salt.

Now increase the heat back to medium and gently stir and cook the rice until all the water is absorbed. Pour in the saffron milk and stir in the almonds, sultanas and sugar. Cover very tightly and put the pan in the oven for 30 minutes.

Remove the rice from the oven and stir, removing the cardamom and cinnamon as you do so. Spoon into a warmed serving dish and gently arrange some silver leaf on the top, if you like. Sprinkle with the extra sultanas and almonds to serve.

Chapatis

Rajbiar Aulakh, London

Makes 4

Chapati-making is a bit of a dying art in Britain today, especially for busy, working parents. Besides, ready-made chapatis are easy enough to buy. But nothing makes a meal feel more Indian than freshly baked chapatis, soft, hot and pliable, torn and used to scoop up everything from chunks of chicken curry to a semi-liquid dal.

Chapatis are cooked on a hot cast-iron griddle known as a tawa and are made with finely ground wholemeal flour (this is sold as 'atta' in Indian grocery stores). It is important to keep the dough as soft as you can manage, so the chapati remains pliable.

135g (scant 5oz) wholemeal flour (atta), plus more to dust
pinch of salt
1 teaspoon olive or sunflower oil

Tip the flour into a bowl and sprinkle in the salt. Make a well in the centre and add the oil. Sift the flour through your fingers to incorporate the oil throughout, then pour in about 100ml (3½fl oz) of lukewarm water, or enough to form a soft dough. Mix together, knead well and make the dough into a smooth ball. Cover with a damp cloth and leave for 30 minutes.

Place the ball of dough on a floured work surface. Knead well for three or four minutes, working the dough hard, then divide it into four equal balls. Set those you are not working with back under the damp cloth, so they don't dry out.

Take a ball of dough and flatten it into an even patty. On a floured work surface, roll it out to 17 centimetres (7 inches) in diameter and 2mm (less than 1/8 inch) thick, rubbing in flour on each side during the process to prevent it from sticking either to the rolling pin or to the work surface.

Make a small wad with a tea towel and keep it close to hand.

Set an Indian tawa or medium-sized cast-iron frying pan over a medium-high heat. When it is hot, lay the chapati flat in your palm and flop it on to the tawa or pan, making sure it lies evenly on the hot surface. Leave it to cook for about 15 seconds, then flip it over.

Take your wadded tea towel and gently press down on the edges of the chapati to ensure they cook through. Also press over any darker uncooked patches. You will notice that small bubbles of steam form within the bread. If you press down, the bubbles will coalesce and the chapati will puff up completely.

Alternatively, if you have a gas cooker, you can flip the chapati directly from the pan on to the flame. Again the chapati will puff up, but from one side only (you'll have to flip it to find the correct side). Overall cooking time for either method is only about one minute. Repeat to cook all the chapatis.

Serve the chapatis as soon as they are made, or stack them in a tea towel-lined basket or on a plate and keep them covered. They should be eaten while they are hot.

Tangy rice pancakes (khatta puda)

Naina Parmar, Leicester

Makes 6, serves 3

These pancakes are a simpler version of 'dosa', the widely eaten pancakes from South India (see page 168). They have a spongy texture and tangy taste and go very well with Naina's Sweet Mango Curry (see page 112). Eat them as you might eat a chapati at any Indian meal, or use them to roll up Indian dishes such as Fenugreek Chicken (see page 79).

200g (7oz) rice flour
12 tablespoons Greek-style
*   yogurt*
½ teaspoon salt
1 teaspoon peeled, finely
*   grated root ginger*
1 teaspoon very finely sliced
*   hot green chilli*
1 teaspoon very finely chopped
*   garlic*
1 tablespoon finely chopped
*   coriander leaves*
about 4 tablespoons olive or
*   sunflower oil*

Put the rice flour in a bowl. Add the yogurt and blend lightly with your fingers. Slowly stir in 250ml (9fl oz) of cool water, mixing thoroughly and leaving no lumps. Leave to ferment in a warm place overnight, or for up to six hours. The batter should have the consistency of single cream. Add the salt, ginger, chilli, garlic and chopped coriander. Stir well.

Set a large non-stick frying pan, about 18 centimetres (7 inches) in diameter, over a medium heat. Check to see if it is hot by dropping in a tiny bit of batter; it should sizzle and stick to the pan immediately. Oil the pan lightly with a piece of oil-soaked kitchen paper.

Pour in 120ml (4fl oz) of the batter and immediately tilt the pan, twisting and turning to allow maximum coverage as the batter spreads evenly to 18–20 centimetres (7–8 inches) in diameter. The pancake will immediately start to steam and to release small bubbles of moisture that will pockmark the surface; this shows that the batter has fermented. The pancake shouldn't be too thin or it will become brittle. Cook for 1–1½ minutes.

Drizzle or brush a little oil on top. The pancake should lift off easily in one piece, revealing an even, golden surface. Flip over and cook for a further 1–1½ minutes. Serve the pancakes piping hot, as quickly as you can make them.

Fried puffed breads (bhatura/padora)

Mahesh Chandra Joshi, Mister Singh's Restaurant, Glasgow

Makes 8

These delicious puffed-up fried breads are rather like pooris, for those who are familiar with them, with just one main difference: they use leavening. This gives them a little more texture. You may make them with wholemeal flour if you wish. I have always known these breads as bhaturas but, in Scotland, I learnt that they are also known as padoras. They are a great favourite with children and adults alike and are particularly good with spicy chickpeas or other beans and vegetables. At Mister Singh's, they are served with a haggis curry.

It helps a great deal if one person rolls the bread and another fries them. I have always enrolled my children, and now my grandchildren, in the rolling. They love to do it and the process moves along with great speed!

260g (9½oz) plain flour, plus more to dust
1 teaspoon baking powder
8 tablespoons yogurt
½ teaspoon salt
1 teaspoon olive or sunflower oil, plus more to oil and to deep-fry

Put the flour and baking powder into a large bowl and mix well. Add all the remaining ingredients and mix to create a loose, crumbly dough. Pour in a small amount of water, about 2 tablespoons, and knead to create a smooth dough ball. Apply a little oil to the palms of your hands and continue to knead until the ball is smooth and shiny. Cover with a damp cloth and leave to rest for 40 minutes.

Set a large karhai, wok or deep, sturdy pan for deep-frying over a medium heat, pour in the oil and allow it to get hot.

Meanwhile, divide the dough into eight equal-sized balls, each about 5 centimetres (2 inches) in diameter.

Flatten a ball of dough, then roll it out on a floured work surface to about 13 centimetres (5 inches) in diameter and about 2mm (less than ⅛ inch) thick.

Carefully slip the bhatura or padora into the hot oil. After a few seconds it will rise up to the surface. Keep pushing it down gently with quick motions, using a slotted spoon, for several seconds, until it puffs up. Turn it over and fry for 20–30 seconds more, until golden brown. Remove and drain on kitchen paper. Make all the bhaturas this way. Serve hot, as soon as you can.

Flatbreads stuffed with potatoes (aloo paratha)

Chaat House, Leicester

Makes 6

Throughout the Punjab, one of the most popular breakfast foods is a stuffed paratha, served with a yogurt raita. There is generally hot, milky, sugared tea in a big glass on the side as well.

As parathas are good travelling food, they often go in children's lunch boxes to school, and in husbands' lunch boxes to the office. Here they may be eaten with some Mango Pickle (see page 178) or some carrot and turnip pickle.

For the stuffing
600g (1lb 4oz) potatoes, par-boiled, peeled and grated
50g (1¾oz) coriander leaves, finely chopped
5 teaspoons finely chopped hot green chilli
1 teaspoon salt

For the parathas
300g (10½oz) chapati flour (or an equal mixture of wholemeal and plain flour), plus more to dust
¼ teaspoon salt
2 teaspoons olive or sunflower oil
3–4 tablespoons melted unsalted butter or ghee

For the stuffing, combine the potatoes, coriander, chilli and salt, ensuring they are evenly mixed. Divide into six equal portions.

To make the parathas, put the flour and salt into a large bowl and pour in the oil. Sift the flour through your fingers to incorporate the oil. Adding about 200ml (7fl oz) of water little by little, combine with your fingertips until you have a moderately soft but elastic dough. Knead well for about five minutes. Shape the dough into a ball and cover with a damp cloth, or place in a plastic bag, and leave to rest for at least 30 minutes. (You may also wrap the dough in cling film and refrigerate it for up to three days at this point.)

Knead the dough once more before forming into six equal balls. Lightly dust a work surface with flour and roll out one ball into an even 13 centimetre (5 inch) round. Take a portion of stuffing and place it centrally on the dough. Pull up the dough around the stuffing until it is completely covered. Twist off the excess dough at the top of the ball and pinch it over the join, sealing the potato in. Pat the ball between your palms and flatten to a round patty shape.

Spread a little extra flour on the work surface and roll the patty out very gently and evenly, to a 16 centimetre (6½ inch) diameter. It doesn't matter if the dough occasionally breaks; simply sprinkle a little extra flour over the split and roll over it gently.

Recipe continued overleaf

Set an Indian tawa or cast-iron frying pan over a medium-high heat and allow it to become hot. Place the paratha on one palm and flop it on to the hot tawa, ensuring it lies flat and is in full contact with the metal. Leave it to cook for one minute before flipping on to the other side. Coat the hot surface with the melted butter or ghee, using the back of a spoon. After one minute flip over once more, again coating the hot exposed surface with more butter or ghee. Flip and coat two or three more times until the paratha is beautifully browned all over. Remove to a plate. Make all the parathas this way.

Parathas may be eaten as they are made, hot and crisp from the tawa, or you can stack them on a large plate or in a basket and cover with a tea towel to keep them warm. Leftover parathas should be allowed to cool, then wrapped in foil and placed in the refrigerator. They can be reheated in a dry frying pan over a medium heat.

Southern savoury pancakes (dosa)

Anita Kara, London

Makes 16

These are not the large, paper-thin fantasies served in South Indian restaurants that seem to get larger annually. They are everyday, home-style dosas (pancakes), yet the pride of South India, eaten at breakfast, lunch and snack time. As they are made with a batter of fermented split peas and rice, they are nutritious and very easy to digest. Today, South Indian restaurants serving dosas can be found in many areas of Britain. And many British Asian families make them at home.

Dosas may be eaten plain with Coconut Chutney and Tomato Chutney (see pages 182 and 188), or filled with their traditional spicy Potato Filling (see page 170), when they are called masala dosas. You may make them for children and fill them with anything you like. Anita often adds cheese, or you may use the potato filling, just leave out the green chillies if you want a masala dosa without heat.

For masala dosas, make the filling before cooking the dosas.

As with crêpes, there is a knack to spreading out the batter that is easy to master with a little practice. Please read the recipe carefully before proceeding, making sure you have everything you need. It takes six to eight hours or overnight to soak the rice and dal, and another 24 hours to allow it to ferment. Once the batter is ready, dosas can be made any time, as it can be refrigerated for two to three days. It may also be frozen.

150g (5½oz) hulled and split
   urad dal
1 teaspoon fenugreek seeds
500g (1lb 2oz) Thai jasmine
   rice
1 teaspoon salt
olive or sunflower oil, to cook

Wash the dal well. Drain. Add the fenugreek seeds and soak in 350ml (12fl oz) of water for six to eight hours, or overnight. Wash the rice well. Drain. Soak it in 700ml (1¼ pints) of water for six to eight hours, or overnight.

Drain the dal, but save the soaking water. Put the dal in a powerful blender or food processor. Add 4 tablespoons of the soaking water and blend for about five minutes, being sure to push down any dal stuck on the sides and to push out any stuck to the bottom of the blender near the blades. Add another 3–4 tablespoons of water and process for another five minutes, or until you have a thick, light cake-like batter. It should be smooth between your fingers. Transfer to a large bowl.

Drain the rice, but save the soaking water. Put the rice in the same blender (you do not need to clean it). Add 240ml (8½fl oz) of the saved water and blend for five minutes. Again, you will need to push the rice down from the sides and make sure that no rice has collected around the blades. Add another 50ml (2fl oz) of the saved water and blend for another five minutes. You will end up with a slightly thinner pancake-like batter. The texture of the rice batter will not be as smooth as the dal batter, and it will feel ever so slightly grainy.

Pour the rice batter into the dal batter. Stir to mix. Leave the bowl, uncovered, in a warm place to ferment for 20–24 hours. Do not disturb it. (I leave mine inside my microwave oven.)

The next day you will see that the batter has risen and it will have bubbles in it. Add the salt and stir it in gently.

When you're ready to cook, assemble a ladle (a flattish-bottomed ladle is best), a measuring cup, some oil, a teaspoon, a rubber spatula, a thin wooden spatula or fish slice and the batter.

Set a 25 centimetre (10 inch) non-stick frying pan over a medium heat. When it's hot, rub the surface with a piece of kitchen paper soaked in oil. Using a measuring cup, pour 120ml (scant 4fl oz) of batter into the centre of the pan and, using the back of the ladle and a very light, hovering touch, push the top of the batter out in concentric circles until the pancake is as thin as possible and about 18 centimetres (7 inches) or a bit more in diameter. Drizzle about 1 teaspoon of oil on top of the dosa and another teaspoon around its outer edge. Spread out the oil and smooth the ridges on the dosa with the rubber spatula. Cook for two minutes, or until the dosa is golden-red on the underside. The outer edges will have loosened from the pan and turned up a bit. If not, loosen them with the thin wooden spatula or fish slice and flip the dosa over. Cook the second side for 50 seconds or so. The dosa is now ready to be served.

Make as many dosas as you like this way. If you wish to make masala dosas (see page 170 for the filling), put the filling along the centre of the dosa and roll it up.

Potato filling for masala dosa

Chennai Sangeetha Restaurant, London

Serves 4

If you wish to make a masala dosa (a stuffed dosa), make this stuffing first. After a dosa is made, lay one-quarter of it along the centre of the dosa and roll it up. Serve Coconut Chutney and Tomato Chutney (see pages 182 and 188) on the side.

600g (1lb 4oz) potatoes
4 tablespoons olive or
*   sunflower oil*
½ teaspoon hulled and split
*   urad dal*
1 teaspoon mustard seeds
30 fresh curry leaves
1 large onion, chopped
¾ teaspoon salt
½ teaspoon turmeric
4–6 green chillies, finely sliced
2 teaspoons peeled, finely
*   grated root ginger*

Boil the potatoes until tender. Drain and peel them, then semi-crush them with a fork or potato masher.

Set a karhai, wok or pan, about 20 centimetres (8 inches) in diameter, over a medium heat. Pour in the oil and, when it's hot, add the urad dal. Stir and fry for a few seconds until the grains turn a shade darker. Add the mustard seeds. Allow them to pop, then drop in the curry leaves. Stir and fry for 30 seconds. Add the onion and stir and fry for about five minutes, until the pieces are translucent.

Now pour in 120ml (scant 4fl oz) of water. Cover, reduce the heat to low and cook for about 10 minutes, stirring now and then, until the onion softens completely. Add the salt, turmeric, chillies and ginger. Mix well for two minutes. Make sure that all the liquid has evaporated, then add the potatoes. Fold them in, making sure they are completely incorporated with the spices.

Salads, pickles, chutneys and relishes

Himalayan salad

Pemba Lama, Basingstoke

Serves 3–4

Nepal lies between two giant countries: China and India. Not surprisingly, its cuisine is influenced by both. This salad is flavoured with Szechuan pepper on the one hand and with chillies, turmeric and fenugreek on the other. Many varieties of the slightly numbing Szechuan pepper, a member of the rue family, are found throughout Nepal, Sikkim and Bhutan. It is also used in India, in the Konkan region of the west coast, where the Chinese once traded. Generally it is only the hull or husk that is crushed and added to foods.

 The Nepalese like to cook their fenugreek seeds until they are dark and bitter. You may cook them for a shorter time, if you prefer.

 This light, pleasant salad may be served with many Indian and Western meals as well.

200g (7oz) white cabbage, shredded
salt, to taste
50g (1¾oz) red onion, finely sliced
50g (1¾oz) carrot, peeled and shredded
100g (3½oz) long, white radish (mooli), peeled and shredded
1 tablespoon finely sliced spring onion, green part only
1 hot red chilli, deseeded and shredded
1 hot green chilli, deseeded and shredded
juice of 1 lemon
10 red, or any, Szechuan peppercorns
1 dried hot chilli
2 teaspoons mustard oil
5–6 fenugreek seeds
¼ teaspoon turmeric
2 tablespoons coriander leaves, to serve

Put the cabbage in a bowl. Add 2 teaspoons of salt and cover with water. Mix well and leave for two minutes, then drain and shake dry.

Combine the cabbage with the red onion, carrot, mooli, spring onion and chillies in a bowl. Squeeze the lemon juice over the top.

Crush the Szechuan peppercorns with the dried chilli and ¼ teaspoon salt to a coarse powder in a mortar and pestle.

Pour the mustard oil into a small pan and set it over a medium heat. When it's hot, add the fenugreek seeds. Fry for two seconds, then add the turmeric. Stir, pour immediately over the salad and toss well. Sprinkle the Szechuan pepper mixture over the top, toss, and sprinkle with coriander to serve.

Prawn salad (prawn bharta)

Tahmima Anam, London

Serves 2

Bengalis, whether they are in Bangladesh, West Bengal or Britain, love the pungent flavour of mustard oil. This delightful salad blends the mustard taste with that of fresh green chillies and fresh green coriander.

Tahmima uses her fingers to massage all the flavours really well into the prawns. This salad is generally eaten with the meal where rice is an important component. It may also be served as a lunchtime salad, or as an an appetiser.

250g (9oz) cooked king prawns, shelled and de-veined
2 shallots, very finely sliced
15g (½oz) coriander leaves, roughly chopped
1–2 hot green chillies, finely sliced
3 spring onions, roughly sliced
1½–2 tablespoons lime juice
2 tablespoons mustard oil (you can substitute a good extra-virgin olive oil, but the flavour will be different)
½–¾ teaspoon salt

Coarsely chop the prawns and place them in a medium-sized bowl. Add all the remaining ingredients and mix well. Check the seasoning for a good balance.

Allow the flavours to mingle and absorb for 10 minutes, then serve.

Nepalese potato salad with a sesame dressing (aloo ko achar)

Kesang Lama, Basingstoke

Serves 4

Kesang is Pemba Lama's talented, young and beautiful daughter who has the same enthusiasm for cookery as her father (for his Himalayan Salad, see page 174). Kesang made this exquisite potato salad for us, saying at the end, 'I would make it much hotter for myself, put in many more green chillies'.

100g (3½oz) frozen peas
500g (1lb 2oz) potatoes,
  boiled, peeled and roughly
  chopped
2 medium carrots, peeled and
  julienned in 5 centimetre
  (2 inch) lengths
1 medium red onion, halved
  and finely sliced
3–6 green chillies, slivered
  lengthways
4 tablespoons sesame seeds,
  roasted and ground
  (see page 219)
¾ teaspoon salt, or to taste
3 tablespoons mustard oil or
  olive oil
¼ teaspoon fenugreek seeds
½ teaspoon turmeric
juice of 1 lemon
1 tablespoon coriander leaves,
  to serve
1 spring onion, green part
  only, shredded, to serve

First bring a saucepan of water to a boil. Add the frozen peas, return to a boil and boil for one minute. Drain, then plunge into cold water to stop the cooking. When cold, drain very well.

Mix the potatoes, carrots, red onion, peas, chillies, ground sesame seeds, salt and peas in a large bowl.

Put the oil in a small frying pan and set it over a medium heat. When it's very hot, add the fenugreek seeds. Five seconds later add the turmeric, stir and quickly pour the oil and seeds over the salad. Add the lemon juice and toss.

Taste for the balance of seasonings, adding more of whatever is needed. Garnish with the coriander and spring onion, then serve.

Mango pickle

Gujarati Rasoi, London

(Makes a 600ml/1 pint jar)

The mangoes needed for pickling are hard, green, unripe and sour; you can find them in Indian grocers. Use 1 large Rajapuri mango, if available, or more if they are smaller; any variety will do. Leave the peel on, but remove the stone. The split mustard seeds used in this recipe, known as mustard dal, are also sold by Indian grocers.

80ml (3fl oz) sunflower oil
1 teaspoon mustard seeds
1 teaspoon ground asafoetida
1 dried red chilli, torn in half
1 tablespoon fenugreek seeds, coarsely crushed
1 teaspoon turmeric
1 teaspoon fennel seeds
1 teaspoon split and skinned mustard seeds (mustard dal)
1 tablespoon salt
500g (1lb 2oz) green mango, chopped into 2 x 1 centimetre (¾ x ½ inch) pieces (see recipe introduction)
1 tablespoon hot chilli powder (or mild, if preferred)

Pour the oil into a large pan about 25 centimetres (10 inches) in diameter and set it over a medium heat. Check to see if the oil is hot by dropping in a mustard seed; it should pop immediately. When the oil is ready, add the asafoetida, remaining mustard seeds and dried chilli. Swirl for 30 seconds, then remove from the heat. Stir in the fenugreek seeds, turmeric, fennel seeds, split mustard seeds and salt. Mix well, then add the mango, stirring to ensuring all the pieces are coated with spice and oil. Allow the pan to cool for five minutes, then mix in the chilli powder, stirring well.

Spoon the pickle into a sterilised jar, pressing down hard to allow the oil to rise up and cover the pickle. Store the jar in a dark, warm place and leave for at least two days. The pickle will be ready for eating but will be crunchy. Given more time the pieces will soften.

If after two or three days there are mango pieces that are still exposed to the air, heat 2–3 tablespoons of oil in a pan. Allow it to cool to warm, then pour it into the jar. As long as the pickle is covered by oil, it will last for up to one year.

Green mango, coconut and cashew nut chutney

Parul Patel, London

(Makes a 450ml/16fl oz jar)

This fresh green chutney may be served with meals or with most fried snacks. The mango must be hard, green, unripe and sour; you will find it at Indian grocers. If you are using a fresh coconut, save the water inside to use in the chutney.

125g (4½oz) peeled, stoned and roughly chopped green mango
60g (2oz) fresh coconut, skinned weight, roughly chopped, or frozen grated coconut, defrosted
60g (2oz) raw cashew nuts
70g (2½oz) coriander leaves
1½ teaspoons salt
1½ teaspoons caster sugar
2 tablespoons reserved coconut water, or just water

Place all the ingredients in a blender and process to a soft paste. Place in a sterilised jar and seal.

Refrigerated, it will keep for a week. This chutney can also be frozen for up to one year.

Mango salsa

Aileen Fernandes, London

Serves 4

This modern Goan salad is part Goan-Indian and part, well, just modern. It may be served with most meals.

400g (14oz) ripe mango, peeled and finely chopped
2 hot green chillies, finely sliced
2 teaspoons olive oil
1 tablespoon lemon juice
½ teaspoon salt

Place the mango in a bowl. Fold in the chillies, olive oil, lemon juice and salt. Serve.

Coconut chutney

Chennai Sangeetha Restaurant, London

(Makes 250ml/9fl oz)

This simple, delicious coconut chutney has a fiery kick, and is the perfect accompaniment for Southern Savoury Pancakes (see page 168). It may be served with most South Asian meals. Keep refrigerated and use within one week.

65g (generous 2oz) freshly grated coconut, or frozen grated coconut, defrosted
2 hot green chillies
1 teaspoon peeled, finely chopped root ginger
¼ teaspoon salt
1 tablespoon olive or sunflower oil
½ teaspoon hulled and split urad dal
½ teaspoon mustard seeds
15 fresh curry leaves, roughly shredded
¼ teaspoon cumin seeds
1 dried chilli

Process the coconut, chillies, ginger and salt in a blender with 4 tablespoons of water. Check for seasoning, then transfer to a small bowl.

Set a small frying pan over a medium heat. Pour in the oil. When it's hot, add the urad dal. Stir and fry for a few seconds until the grains turn light brown. Add the mustard seeds and allow to pop. Drop in the curry leaves and stir for five seconds before adding the cumin seeds. Finally drop in the dried chilli. Stir and fry until it is a shade darker. Pour the whole mixture, with the oil, into the blended coconut and mix well.

Dry coconut chutney

Ganapati Restaurant, London

(Makes 250ml/9fl oz)

Just put this on the dinner table and sprinkle it over rice, or eat with Southern Savoury Pancakes (see page 168).

For many dishes in South India, coconut oil is the usual cooking medium. For this recipe, you may use sunflower oil instead, though the flavour of the finished chutney will be different.

For the chutney
1 tablespoon coconut oil, or sunflower oil (see recipe introduction)
2 shallots, roughly chopped
2 tablespoons peeled, finely grated root ginger
1 garlic clove, roughly chopped
1 teaspoon chilli powder
12 fresh curry leaves
90g (3¼oz) freshly grated coconut, or frozen grated coconut, defrosted, plus 1 tablespoon

For the tarka
2 teaspoons coconut oil, or sunflower oil (see recipe introduction)
1 teaspoon mustard seeds

Place the oil, shallots, ginger, garlic, chilli powder, curry leaves and the 1 tablespoon of grated coconut in a blender and grind to a paste. Mix in the remaining grated coconut.

Set a medium-sized pan, about 15 centimetres (6 inches) in diameter, over a medium heat. When it's hot, pour in the 2 teaspoons of coconut oil and let it heat up. Add the mustard seeds and allow to pop. Reduce the heat and add the coconut mixture. Stir and fry for three minutes until thoroughly mixed and somewhat drier but still moist.

Fresh coriander chutney

Sarojini Gulhane, London

Serves 4

A good vitamin-rich chutney that is served with most meals throughout India. This can act like a base as well, mixing wonderfully well with yogurt for dips, or as a rub for fish, or as an enriching ingredient for curry sauces.

60g (2oz) coriander leaves, finely chopped
2 tablespoons roughly chopped hot green chillies
5–6 garlic cloves, roughly chopped
7.5 centimetre (3 inch) peeled root ginger, chopped
½ teaspoon salt
2 tablespoons olive or sunflower oil
¼ teaspoon mustard seeds
¼ teaspoon cumin seeds
4 fresh curry leaves, shredded
pinch of ground asafoetida
2 tablespoons lemon juice

Put one-third of the coriander in a blender (this would be easier in a mini processor) with 1 tablespoon of water and blend to a paste. Add the remaining coriander in batches and process, adding small amounts of water if necessary to make the paste. Mix in the chillies, garlic, ginger and salt and blend again.

Put the oil in a small frying pan and set it over a medium heat. When it's hot, add the mustard seeds. As soon as they have popped, about 15 seconds, add the cumin seeds, curry leaves and asafoetida. After 15 seconds, add the coriander paste. Stir once or twice to mix, then remove from the heat. Transfer to a small bowl and mix in the lemon juice.

Tomato chutney

Chennai Sangeetha Restaurant, London

Makes 600ml/1 pint

This South Indian tomato chutney gets its tartness from tamarind. Serve it with Southern Savoury Pancakes (see page 168), or with Indian meals and snack foods.

For the chutney
6 tablespoons olive or
   sunflower oil
20 fresh curry leaves
4–5 hot dried chillies
6 garlic cloves, roughly
   chopped
2 tablespoons peeled, roughly
   chopped root ginger
4 teaspoons tamarind
   concentrate
2 medium onions, roughly
   chopped
4 medium tomatoes, roughly
   chopped
1 teaspoon salt
70g (2½oz) chana dal

For the tarka
4 teaspoons olive or
   sunflower oil
1 teaspoon mustard seeds
½ teaspoon hulled and split
   urad dal
15 fresh curry leaves
5–6 hot dried chillies
⅛ teaspoon ground asafoetida

Set a small pan, about 18 centimetres (7 inches) in diameter, over a medium heat. Pour in 4 tablespoons of the oil. When it's hot, drop in the curry leaves and stir. Add the dried chillies and stir and fry until they darken a shade. Now tip in the garlic and ginger and stir and fry until the garlic starts to turn brown. Spoon in the tamarind and mix well for one minute.

Add the onions and sauté for two minutes. Mix in the tomatoes and salt and stir for a further two or three minutes until they just start to soften. Remove from the heat.

Set another small pan over a medium heat and pour in the remaining 2 tablespoons of oil. When it's hot, drop in the chana dal. Stir and fry for two or three minutes until all the grains have turned a reddish gold colour. Add all the contents of this pan to the tomato chutney, then scrape it into a blender, or use a stick blender. Blend until smooth, then transfer to a bowl.

Put the oil for the tarka in a small frying pan and set it over a medium-high heat. When it's hot, drop in the mustard seeds and allow to pop, then add the urad dal. Stir and fry until it just starts to darken. Add the curry leaves and dried chillies. Stir and fry until the chilies darken, then remove from the heat and sprinkle in the asafoetida. Pour the contents of the pan into the tomato chutney. Mix well and allow to cool.

Store in the refrigerator and use with one week.

Tamarind chutney

Roti Chai, London

Makes about 250ml/9fl oz

Essential in any chaat (see pages 14 and 202), for its tangy, sour and sparkling flavour.

1 tablespoon tamarind
   concentrate
125g (4½oz) jaggery or dark
   brown sugar
¼ teaspoon ground ginger
½ teaspoon chilli powder
½ teaspoon crushed, roasted
   cumin seeds (see page 219)
1¼ teaspoons chaat masala,
   or to taste
¼–½ teaspoon salt

Pour 170ml (6fl oz) of boiling water into a small pan about 15 centimetres (6 inches) in diameter. Set it over a medium heat and stir in the tamarind. Now stir in the jaggery and dissolve it in the water. When it has dissolved, add the ginger, chilli powder, crushed, roasted cumin seeds and chaat masala. Bring to a boil, then reduce the heat to a simmer. Add the salt and stir.

Simmer to reduce the liquid for about 15 minutes, or until it thickens to a thin syrup. Remove the pan from the heat and cool. The liquid will thicken. Store the chutney in a sterilised jar and keep in a dark, cool place.

Cucumber, onion and mint raita

Rubina Haider, London

Serves 4–6

Raitas – yogurt-based salads – are served with most Indian and Pakistani meals. They add a cooling crunch. They are a standard accompaniment to all biryanis.

250ml (9fl oz) yogurt
100g (3½oz) cucumber,
   coarsely grated
½ medium onion, finely sliced
2 teaspoons finely chopped
   mint
salt, to taste
good pinch of freshly ground
   black pepper

Whisk the yogurt in a bowl. Simply mix in all the other ingredients.

Scoop the raita into a serving bowl.

Beetroot raita

Sumayya Jamal, London

Serves 4–6

A vivid, vibrant raita that uses jaggery. Use a soft molasses-rich sugar as an alternative.

250ml (9fl oz) yogurt
90g (3¼oz) beetroot, grated
1 teaspoon cumin seeds,
   toasted and crushed
   (see page 219)
jaggery or sugar, to taste
sea salt, to taste
1 hot green chilli, finely sliced
1–2 teaspoons finely chopped
   mint leaves
1 tablespoon finely chopped
   coriander leaves

Whisk the yogurt in a bowl and add the beetroot, cumin, jaggery, salt and chilli.

Scoop the bright pink-tinged raita into a serving bowl and garnish with the mint and coriander.

Drinks and sweets

Lemonade (nimbu pani)

Nikita Gulhane, London

Serves 4

There are many variations of this thirst-quenching drink, which is very popular in all seasons, but its mixture of sweet, salt, sharp and spicy flavours is particularly enjoyed on a hot day. This version is aromatic and tinted with saffron.

2 cloves
seeds from 2 green cardamom pods
12 saffron threads
8 tablespoons freshly squeezed lemon or lime juice
10 teaspoons caster sugar, or to taste
¼ teaspoon salt, or to taste
¼ teaspoon freshly ground black pepper, or to taste
1 litre (1¾ pints) chilled sparkling water

Set a small frying pan over a low heat. When it's hot, add the cloves and cardamom seeds. Heat gently for one minute, stirring frequently. Remove the pan from the heat and sprinkle in the saffron. Stir again and tip out of the pan. When all the spices are cool, grind them to a fine powder. (You may use a mortar and pestle for this.)

Pour the lemon juice into a large jug. Dissolve the sugar in it. Add the salt, black pepper and 4 pinches of the ground spice mixture. Stir well. Drop in ice cubes or crushed ice. Pour in the sparkling water, stir and serve.

Add more sugar, salt or spice mixture to taste.

Salty spiced lassi (taaq)

Sarojini Gulhane, London

Serves 4

Among the many combinations possible for this everyday drink, here is a very aromatic version containing fresh curry leaves. It may be drunk with meals or taken as a snack.

450ml (16fl oz) yogurt
1½ teaspoons caster sugar, or to taste
1 teaspoon salt, or to taste
1 teaspoon finely chopped coriander leaves
1 teaspoon olive or sunflower oil
¼ teaspoon mustard seeds
¼ teaspoon cumin seeds
¼ teaspoon turmeric
3 fresh curry leaves, shredded
½ teaspoon finely chopped or crushed garlic
½ teaspoon peeled, finely chopped root ginger
½ teaspoon finely chopped hot green chilli

Scrape the yogurt into a large bowl and gradually whisk in 500ml (18fl oz) of water, until smooth. Add the sugar, salt and coriander leaves and whisk once more.

Pour the oil into a medium pan and set it over a medium-high heat. When it's hot, add the mustard seeds. As soon as they pop, a matter of seconds, put in the cumin seeds and turmeric, followed by the curry leaves, garlic, ginger and green chilli. Stir for a few seconds, then pour the yogurt mixture into the pan. Stir once, then immediately pour the whole contents of the pan back into the bowl.

Taste for salt and sugar, adding more if you wish. Serve with ice cubes for a refreshing drink, ideally on a very hot day.

Mango-flavoured yogurt drink (mango lassi)

Ganapati Restaurant, London

Serves 2

Use the pulp of fresh mangoes when they are in season to make this cooling, refreshing drink. When fresh mangoes are unavailable, use canned mango pulp. A little ground cardamom may be added, if you wish.

250ml (9fl oz) yogurt
250ml (9fl oz) mango pulp
5 tablespoons whole milk
1 tablespoon caster sugar,
or to taste

Combine all the ingredients in a blender and process to mix well. Taste, adding more sugar if you would like a sweeter drink.

Add ice cubes if you wish, and serve.

Masala chai

Rajbiar Aulakh, London

Serves 4

Masala chai is taken every day in five-star hotels, at home, or sipped while standing beside a road side vendor. There are a zillion variations, some even use black peppercorns for an extra kick. This is Rajbiar's familiy recipe.

2 slices root ginger, each
*   5 x ½ centimetre*
*   (2 x ¼ inch) thick*
1 black cardamom pod
2 green cardamom pods
4 cloves
2 star anise
2.5 centimetre (1 inch)
*   cinnamon stick*
*   or cassia bark*
3 tea bags
250ml (9fl oz) whole milk
caster sugar, to taste

Set a medium-sized pan, about 18 centimetres (7 inches) in diameter, over a medium-high heat. Pour in 750ml (1½ pints) of water and bring to a boil.

Meanwhile, gently crush the ginger, both types of cardamom pod, cloves, star anise and cinnamon in a mortar and pestle. When the water is boiling, add the spices and the tea bags. Reduce the heat to a simmer, cover and simmer for five minutes. Pour in the milk.

Rerturn to a boil, then reduce the heat and simmer for one final minute. Add as much sugar as you like, then serve.

Tangy, spicy fruit salad (fruit chaat)

Roti Chai, London

Serves 4

In India it is not unusual to combine spices with fruit. My mother made fruit chaats for us throughout the year. We usually had them at lunchtime. This fruit chaat can be eaten as an appetiser or palate cleanser before, during or after a meal.

1 small apple
1 banana
½ medium papaya
3 tablespoons of lime juice,
  or to taste
2–3 tablespoons tamarind
  chutney, or to taste
  (see page 192 if you wish to
  make your own)
⅛ teaspoon crushed, roasted
  cumin seeds (see page 219)
12 grapes
4 tablespoons pomegranate
  seeds
8 mint leaves

Peel the apple, banana and papaya. Slice the banana on the diameter and cut the apple and papaya into 2.5 centimetre (1 inch) chunks.

Pour half the lime juice and 1 tablespoon of tamarind chutney into a large bowl. Mix in the crushed, roasted cumin seeds. Toss all the fruits – apple, banana, papaya, grapes and pomegranate seeds – gently in this dressing, ensuring they are all coated. Taste and add more chutney and lime juice as desired.

Divide between four serving bowls and garnish with ripped mint leaves.

Almond and cardamom kulfi

Sheela Junankar, London

Makes 1.4 litres (2½ pints)

This ice cream is a very fast version of the elaborate kulfi that I grew up with as a child. It is the classic Indian ice cream, generally flavoured with pistachios, rose water and almonds. Today, modern British chefs have begun to add new dimensions to it, with lime zest, candied ginger, passion fruit, even pumpkin.

Unlike Western ice cream, kulfi does not need to be churned.

600ml (1 pint) double cream
400ml can condensed milk
340ml can evaporated milk
70g (2½oz) ground almonds
½ teaspoon ground
   cardamom

Pour the double cream into a large bowl and whisk for two to three minutes, until it starts to thicken but not stiffen.

In another large bowl, whisk the condensed and evaporated milks together until smooth. Add the cream, then stir in the ground almonds and cardamom.

Whisk for three to four minutes, then pour into individual moulds. Cover, then freeze for up to one month.

Sweet yogurt 'custard' with cardamom (bhapa doi)

Mallika Basu, London

Serves 6

This is a classic Bengali sweet that customers in India buy from their favourite shops, already set in red clay pots. In Britain, this yogurt custard has to be made at home to satisfy many a Bengali sweet tooth. Here is a quick domestic version that uses many short cuts, including canned condensed milk.

500ml (18fl oz) yogurt
400ml can condensed milk
1 teaspoon ground cardamom
12 saffron threads, soaked in
   2 tablespoons of warm
   whole milk

Preheat the oven to 190°C/375°F/gas mark 5.

Pour the yogurt into a large bowl. Whisk in the condensed milk and the ground cardamom. Boil a full kettle of water.

Divide the yogurt mixture between six ramekins or small bowls, each about 9 centimetres (3½ inches) in diameter and 4½ centimetres (1¾ inches) deep. Place them in a deep ovenproof baking tray or roasting dish.

Open the oven door and, working quickly, slide the baking tray or roasting dish on to the middle shelf. Pull the shelf out to halfway. Now pour hot water from the kettle into the tray or dish, to halfway up the sides of the ramekins, then carefully slide the shelf back in and shut the oven door. Bake for 10 minutes.

Slide out the oven shelf once more and divide the saffron and milk between the ramekins. Slide the shelf back in, close the door and bake for a further 10 minutes.

Remove from the oven and the baking tray or roasting dish. Leave to cool, then eat warm or cold.

Semolina halva (sheera)

Sarojini Gulhane, London

Serves 4

Called suji halva, sheera, seero, shira and many other names, this simple halva is eaten all over India. It is often offered in temples as the food the gods bless before distribution to the masses. It is sometimes eaten plain but may also be eaten with Indian fried puffed breads, pooris. It can be eaten hot and soft, or warm and firm. Typically sultanas are added, but here cranberries provide a tart garnish.

500ml (18fl oz) semi-skimmed milk
seeds from 3 green cardamom pods, ground to a powder
12 saffron threads
80g (3oz) coarse semolina
70g (2½oz) unsalted butter
50g (1¾oz) unrefined soft brown sugar
3 tablespoons ground almonds
4 almonds, finely sliced
1 tablespoon dried cranberries

Bring the milk to a boil in a small pan, reduce the heat to very low and add the cardamom and saffron. Let the milk simmer gently.

Meanwhile, set a karhai, wok or small pan, 18 centimetres (7 inches) in diameter or so, over a medium heat. Pour in the semolina and toast it gently for five to six minutes, stirring all the while to make sure it doesn't burn.

Now add the butter and sugar and mix well for one minute to form a thick paste. Pour in the hot milk, stirring all the while, then increase the heat and bring to a boil. Add the ground almonds, mixing thoroughly for one minute, then reduce the heat to medium-low and cover. After two minutes, uncover and stir well. Cover again and cook for another two minutes.

Transfer the sheera to a serving dish and serve garnished with the sliced almonds and cranberries.

Coconut barfi

Kalwant Sahota, London

Makes 15 pieces

A barfi is an Indian sweetmeat very often made with a base of khoya: milk that has been boiled and reduced to a doughy thickness. Kalwant's version of this Indian sweet uses a clever short cut: condensed milk. Despite the lack of sugar, it is very sweet. Barfi is made in many different flavours; here it is coconut. As an extra treat omit the coconut coating and dunk half the barfi in melted chocolate, allowing it to set before serving.

7 tablespoons condensed milk
10 saffron threads, soaked in
   ½ teaspoon warm water.
seeds from 6 green cardamom
   pods, crushed in a mortar
   and pestle
100g (3½oz) desiccated
   coconut, blended to a coarse
   powder, plus more to coat

Pour the condensed milk into a small, preferably non-stick pan about 18 centimetres (7 inches) in diameter and set it over a medium heat. Warm it for two minutes, then stir in the saffron and its water. Sprinkle in the cardamom and stir for one minute, then add the coconut, incorporating it thoroughly and quickly into a thick, sticky paste. Stir continuously until the mixture pulls away from the sides of the pan in a ball.

Remove from the heat and cool until it is comfortable to touch. With wet hands, take small pieces of the mixture, each about the size of a large hazelnut, and roll into a ball. Dredge each ball in coconut powder to coat it well and store in an airtight container for up to two weeks.

Spiced banana tarte Tatin

Vivek Singh, The Cinnamon Club, London

Serves 4–6

Here is a modern dessert in the 'fusion' style. It is basically French, but with Indian flavours. Vivek recommends using the very small, stubby bananas available in Asian stores, but any will do. His favourite accompaniment is vanilla ice cream dusted with ground cinnamon.

For the caramel
150g (5½oz) caster sugar
15g (½oz) unsalted butter

For the tarte Tatin
a little cooking oil
4 bananas
*½ tsp pink peppercorns,
    coarsely crushed, plus more
    to garnish (optional)*
*200g (7oz) ready-rolled puff
    pastry, preferably all-butter*

Grease a 25 centimetre (10 inch) tart tin with some cooking oil. Preheat the oven to 170°C/340°F/gas mark 3½.

Put a small, heavy-based pan, 15 centimetres (6 inches) in diameter, over a medium heat. Pour in half the sugar. Heat and, as it starts to melt, add the remaining sugar in batches, stirring to mix the liquid sugar with the solid. Cook until all the sugar is liquid and light brown. Add the butter, stir and remove from the heat. The sugar will continue to cook and turn a nutty brown colour. Pour the caramel into the tart tin and tilt to spread it out evenly. Allow to cool.

Peel and slice the bananas evenly, on the diagonal, about ½ centimetre (¼ inch) thick. Arrange them in overlapping circles over the set caramel, covering it completely. Sprinkle the crushed peppercorns on top. Lay the puff pastry over the tart tin and cut to fit generously over the bananas. Gently push it down with a blunt knife between the rim of the tin and the bananas to create a snug fit.

Place the tart on the middle shelf of the hot oven. Bake for about 20 minutes, or until the pastry puffs up and turns a golden brown. Remove from the oven.

Run a knife around the edge of the tart tin, then cover the tin with a plate and invert. Prise out and carefully replace any stray pieces of banana that stick to the tin. Garnish with extra pink peppercorns to taste, if you like. Serve hot, or warm, with ice cream.

Spice mixes

Spice mixes

Every family mixes its own spices in the South Asian subcontinent. This tradition has been maintained by many of the Indians and Pakistanis who have migrated to Britain, but an equal number buy blends from grocery stores.

For example, garam masala, a mix of aromatic spices that heat the body, is a common blend that many people in the UK just buy. On the other hand, as I was collecting recipes all over Britain, I found that quite a few of them required special, home-made blends that gave their own unique flavour to the dishes. All of you cooking from this book have a choice: you can either buy a general garam masala or chaat masala from a shop when it is called for, or you can make the specific blend the original recipe required. Each recipe in question will give you the choice. You might need to go to an Indian grocer for some of these ingredients.

Here are some special blends that you can choose from:

My garam masala
Makes 3 tablespoons

This is the garam masala that is used in my family. It is very strong and aromatic. You can buy the cardamom seeds, already podded, from Indian grocers.

> 1 tablespoon green cardamom seeds
> 1 teaspoon black peppercorns
> 1 teaspoon black cumin seeds
> 1 teaspoon cloves
> 5 centimetre (2 inch) piece cassia bark or
>   cinnamon stick, broken up
> 1/3 whole nutmeg

Put all the spices in a clean coffee grinder, or other spice grinder, and grind as finely as possible, in batches if necessary. Store in a small, tightly lidded jar in a cool, dark place.

Vivek's garam masala
Vivek Singh, The Cinnamon Club, London
Makes 70g (2½oz)

Vivek's garam masala is a particularly fragrant mixture and almost a tale of two ancient cultures. The star anise is native to China and, combined with the fennel seeds, gives a strong aroma of aniseed. The green cardamom pods are South Asian and add an aromatic softness.

> 12 star anise
> 15 centimetre (6 inch) piece cinnamon
>   stick or cassia bark
> 18 green cardamom pods
> 6 teaspoons fennel seeds

Set a small pan, karhai or wok over a medium heat. When it's hot, add the star anise, cinnamon and cardamom pods. Stir constantly for 30 seconds, then add the fennel seeds. Stir for a further 20–30 seconds. Empty out on to a plate to cool.

Put all the spices in a clean coffee grinder, or other spice grinder, and grind as finely as possible, in batches if necessary. Store in a small, tightly lidded jar in a cool, dark place.

Chaat House's special garam masala

Chaat House, Leicester

Makes 70g (2½oz)

The use of star anise is quite unusual here, as is the addition of so many cloves.

> 4–5 cassia leaves
> 5 black cardamom pods
> 10–15 green cardamom pods
> 4 tablespoons black peppercorns
> 1½ tablespoons cloves
> 4–5 star anise
> 3–4 blades of mace

Put all the spices in a clean coffee grinder, or other spice grinder, and grind as finely as possible, in batches if necessary. Store in a small, tightly lidded jar in a cool, dark place.

Yesmien's garam masala

Yesmien Bagh Ali, Skipton, Yorkshire

Makes 65g (2¼oz)

A nicely aromatic, basic blend.

> 4 tablespoons cumin seeds
> 4 tablespoons coriander seeds
> 1 teaspoon cloves
> 1 tablespoon black peppercorns
> 5 centimetre (2 inch) piece cinnamon stick, broken up
> 6 cassia leaves or bay leaves, broken up
> 3 black cardamom pods

Put all the spices in a clean coffee grinder, or other spice grinder, and grind as finely as possible, in batches if necessary. Store in a small, tightly lidded jar in a cool, dark place.

Naina's garam masala

Naina Parmar, Leicester

Makes about 115g (4oz)

This interesting garam masala contains two types of peppercorn, ground ginger and asafoetida, which makes it quite unusual.

> 1 tablespoon coarsely ground cassia bark or cinnamon stick
> 1 tablespoon cloves
> 2 teaspoons white peppercorns
> 2 teaspoons black peppercorns
> 1 tablespoon ground ginger
> ½ teaspoon ground asafoetida

Put all the spices in a clean coffee grinder, or other spice grinder, and grind as finely as possible, in batches if necessary. Store in a small, tightly lidded jar in a cool, dark place.

Gurdwara's special garam masala

Southall Gurdwara, London

Makes 80g (3oz)

This is a nice, cheap blend because of the use of cumin and coriander. These are really fillers, not true garam masalas.

> 5 teaspoons coriander seeds
> 5 teaspoons cumin seeds
> 5 teaspoons black peppercorns
> 5 black cardamom pods
> 10 cassia leaves or bay leaves, broken up
> 25 centimetre (10 inch) piece cassia bark, broken up

Put all the spices in a clean coffee grinder, or other spice grinder, and grind as finely as possible, in batches if necessary. Store in a small, tightly lidded jar in a cool, dark place.

Yesmien's basaar mix

Yesmien Bagh Ali, Skipton, Yorkshire
Makes 110g (scant 4oz)

This is a very red Kashmiri spice mix, its colour
the result of the chilli powder that is its main
ingredient. Think of it as a flavoured chilli
powder. It is used by many of the Pakistani
Kashmiris who settled in Yorkshire. It is best to
wear plastic gloves while making this.

> 50g (1¾oz) hot chilli powder (or mild chilli
>   powder, if you prefer)
> 25g (scant 1oz) paprika
> 2 teaspoons turmeric
> 1½ teaspoons ground coriander
> 1½ teaspoons ground cumin
> 1¼ teaspoons garam masala (ideally
>   Yesmien's Garam Masala, see page 215)
> ¾ teaspoon ground fenugreek
> 1 tablespoon dried fenugreek leaves
>   (kasuri methi)
> ⅛ teaspoon ground asafoetida
> 4 teaspoons mustard oil

Mix all the ingredients except the oil together in
a large bowl. Drizzle in the oil.

Now rub the oil into the spice powders. Yesmien
likes to take her time over this task, anything up
to 15 minutes. Like her, you may wish to wear
latex gloves to avoid tainting your skin with
chilli, or with mustard oil. Store in an airtight
container, away from heat and sunlight.

Yesmien's chaat masala

Yesmien Bagh Ali, Skipton, Yorkshire
Makes 22g (¾oz)

Black rock salt is a digestive that is used in many
Indian spice combinations to add an unique,
slightly pungent, almost sulphurous flavour.
Very small quantities are put into chaat masala,
the spice mixture used for the hot and sour
snack foods that are known generally as 'chaat'.

> 1 teaspoon ground cumin
> 1 teaspoon ground coriander
> 1 teaspoon black salt
> ½ teaspoon ordinary salt
> ¾ teaspoon ground ginger
> ½ teaspoon freshly ground black pepper
> ¼ teaspoon hot chilli powder
> 2 tablespoons ground amchoor (green mango
>   powder)

Mix all the ground spices together. Store in a
small, tightly lidded jar in a cool, dark place.

Seasonings, techniques and kitchen equipment

Seasonings

There are certain fresh seasonings that appear again and again in South Asian foods. These include garlic, root ginger, fresh green coriander, fresh curry leaves, and fresh green chillies.

Coriander, fresh: When you buy the bunch of herbs, wrap it up, unwashed, in kitchen paper and then put it in a tightly closed, flat plastic container. Store in the refrigerator. Take out the amount you need and wash it well. Use just the top leaves and top sprigs for garnishing but, if you are cooking with it, you may use a good three-quarters of the plant. Just remember to cut the stems across into very, very small bits.

Curry leaves, fresh: It has taken Britain a very short span of its history to take to curry. Curry leaves will not be far behind. They give such a sunny aroma to southern and coastal foods that even I, a northern girl who grew up not knowing curry leaves, have now fallen under their spell. Ask, no demand, that your local grocer carry them. It will happen. Curry leaves, used for their aroma and flavour, are either just put into fish stews or dals as they are cooking, or they are used in the 'tarka'. But more about the 'tarka' later.

Garlic: This is often required to form the base of a curry sauce, along with onions, ginger and sometimes tomatoes. It should be peeled and then crushed either in a garlic press, or in a mortar with a pestle. Some people actually grate it on a Microplane. Others freeze it for future use in small ice cube trays, a teaspoon's worth in a compartment. These little blobs, when frozen, can be transferred to polythene bags and kept in the freezer.

Ginger, root: Follow the directions for garlic. Peel and then grate on a medium Microplane, or grind in a mini food processor, until you have a pulp. Freeze in the same manner as the garlic.

Green chillies, hot, fresh: Indians like their chillies thin, long and of medium-high heat (no, not the scorchers such as the habanero). All Indian grocers carry them. As you cannot always know how hot a chilli is, just break it in the centre and smell it. This will give you a good indication. Otherwise, take the tiniest bite. A chilli is hottest at the stem end and least hot at the tip. That is why testing it in the middle is best. Green chillies give a very fresh taste to vegetables, dals, snacks, and salads and are thus used in great quantities.

Techniques

The tarka: This is a special technique used in Indian cooking to blast a heightened, caramelised, spicy flavour into bland dals, vegetables and even meat and fish dishes. It is usually done at the start of the cooking or at the end, using spices that are generally whole. If you were cooking a dal or a dried bean dish, you might just boil it until it is tender and then add some salt. So far, the dish could belong to any country. Then you would take a very small frying pan and put a few tablespoons of oil or ghee (clarified butter) into it. When it is hot you might put in cumin seeds, a whole dried chilli and a few slices of garlic. Once the garlic is golden, you would empty the contents of the little frying pan into the cooked dal or beans and close the lid to keep the aromas in. This is a tarka. It changes a dish from bland to exciting.

Roasting spices and seeds: If roasted and ground spices are called for, put them a small cast-iron frying pan over a medium-high heat. Stir and roast until they are a few shades darker and smell roasted. Then grind in a clean coffee grinder or other spice grinder. What is not needed may be stored in a tightly lidded jar.

Roasting aubergine flesh: Many recipes call for roasted aubergines. In the Indian and Pakistani states of the Punjab, many homes have a tandoor oven going all the time. Large aubergines are just left in the hot ashes to roast. When they are soft, the ashen skin is peeled off and the pulp used in all manner of dishes. In the rest of India, wood and charcoal braziers are used the same way. In Britain, where most people have just their hobs, ovens and grills, the same roasting is done in many other ways.

1. Top-of-the-hob method for a gas cooker: This is a somewhat messy job, so line your burner with foil. Pick an aubergine with a stem. Prick it with a fork so it won't burst. Stand it up on a low gas flame, holding it with a pair of tongs. When the bottom is charred, lay the aubergine down. Move it as needed until one side is completely charred. Now turn the aubergine a little bit until the adjacent section chars. Keep turning until the entire vegetable is charred. Hold it carefully by the stem end at this stage or it might come apart. A 675g (1lb 7oz) aubergine will take 35–40 minutes to cook. Peel and rinse quickly to remove any bits of charred skin. Pat dry. This aubergine will have a lovely, smoky flavour.

2. The oven-roasting method: This is good when you have many aubergines to roast or have an electric cooker. Preheat the oven to 230°C/450°F/gas mark 8. Prick the aubergines with a fork and lay them in a baking tray lined with foil. Roast, turning every 15 minutes. Aubergines weighing 450g (1lb) will take an hour. They will flatten and turn very soft. They will not have the smoky flavour.

Kitchen equipment

You will notice that I often give the exact dimensions of pans used in my recipes. You do not have to follow it to the letter. It is just to let you know the size I used, as I thought it best, and that the timings are based on that size. A larger pot might mean that something browns faster and a smaller pot might imply that you have to cook for longer. Just use your own judgement.

No special equipment is needed to make Indian food, though a blender (or mini food processor) and spice grinder are important. A well-equipped kitchen should have everything Indian cooking requires. I like Microplanes of varying sizes to grate and grind.

You might find that the measurements are a bit inconsistent. I just made different decisions with each recipe, depending upon when an exact measurement was crucial and when it was not.

Index

aduki bean curry 126
almond and cardamom kulfi 204
aloo gobi 108
aloo gosht 41
aloo ko achar 176
aloo paratha 165–7
aubergines 219
  aubergine with nigella seeds 102
  fire-roasted aubergines with curry leaves 105
  fire-roasted aubergines with garlic and tomatoes 104
  Madhur's hot and sour aubergine 102
  stuffed aubergines 106
  see also Onion Bhajias

bananas
  spiced banana tarte tatin 210
basaar mix, Yesmien's 216
beans
  aduki bean curry 126
  potato and long bean curry 122
  spicy chickpeas, potatoes and beans in a tamarind sauce 14
  sprouted mung bean salad 16
  yogurt sauce with broad beans 136
beef
  minty beef meatballs 62–3
beetroot
  beetroot raita 193
  lamb with beetroot 42
bhapa doi 206
bharta (versions I and II) 104, 105
bhatura 164
bhindi gosht 30

biryani
  chicken biryani 155–7
  Lahore lamb biryani 152–4
biscuits
  fried savoury biscuits 17
black dal 130
  mixed black dal 128
boatman's curry 92
breads
  chapatis 160–1
  flatbreads stuffed with potatoes 165–7
  fried puffed breads 164
broad beans
  yogurt sauce with broad beans 136
butteta ne methi 118

cashew nut and curry leaf rice 146
cauliflower
  cauliflower with potatoes 108
  see also Onion Bhajias
chaat masala 216
chaats 14
chana aloo chaat 14
chana dal cooked with mung dal 131
chapatis 160–1
chhole 132
chicken
  chicken biryani 155–7
  chicken in a coconut sauce 70
  chicken in a wok 69
  chicken kebabs 26
  chicken with cream (chicken malaidar) 72–3
  chicken with spinach (chicken palag) 74
  fenugreek chicken 79
  green masala minced chicken 68
  Madhur's chicken tikka masala 76–8
  Nagore chicken curry 83
  pan-roasted whole chicken with carom seeds 80
  rice cooked with chicken in an aromatic chicken broth 150
  whole roasted masala chicken 82
chickpea flour spread 135
chickpeas
  chickpeas with tomato 132

spicy chickpeas, potatoes and beans in
a tamarind sauce 14
chilli mutton chops (chilli champ) 28
chillies, green 218
chukandar gosht 42
chutneys
coconut chutney 182
dry coconut chutney 184
fresh coriander chutney 187
green mango, coconut and cashew nut chutney
181
tamarind chutney 192
tomato chutney 188
coconut barfi 208
coconut chutney 182
dry coconut chutney 184
coconut rice 143
cod
fish in a Bengali-style sauce 98
coley
fish balls in masala (fish kofte) 91
coriander 218
fresh coriander chutney 187
cucumber, onion and mint raita
193
curry leaves 218
cashew nut and curry leaf rice 146

dals
aduki bean curry 126
black dal 130
chana dal cooked with mung dal 131
chickpeas with tomato 132
dal fritters (dal vadas) 21
mixed black dal 128
red lentil and chana dal 138
rice and mung dal 149
rice with toor dal and vegetables 148–9
split pea and tomato sauce with noodles
(dal dhokri) 30–3
dhora 26
dosa 168–9

egg curry 66

fenugreek
fenugreek chicken 79
potatoes with fresh fenugreek 118
fish
boatman's curry 92
fish balls in masala (fish kofte) 91
fish in a Bengali-style sauce 98
Keralan fish curry 97
seared halibut with Bengal dopiyaza sauce 94–6
flatbreads stuffed with potatoes 165–7
fried puffed breads 164
fritters
dal fritters (dal vadas) 21
tapioca pearl fritters (sabudana vadas) 20
fruit
tangy, spicy fruit salad (fruit chaat) 202

garam masala 214–5
garlic 218
Ghurka-style pork curry with choi sum 56–8
ginger, root 218
Goan pork vindaloo with potatoes 60
Goan prawn curry 86
gram flour
chickpea flour spread 135
green mango, coconut and cashew nut chutney
181
green masala minced chicken 68
ground greens in the Punjabi style 110
Gujarati vegetable samosas 25

halibut
seared halibut with Bengal dopiyaza sauce 94–6
hare masala ka chicken keema 68
Himalayan salad 174

kachche murgh ki biryani 155–7
kadhi 136
kale cooked in an East African style 116
karhai chicken 69
Kashmiri-style rich lamb curry 46
Keralan fish curry 97
khara masala gosht 45

khatta puda 162
khichri (versions I and II) 148–9
kidney beans
    spicy chickpeas, potatoes and beans in
        a tamarind sauce 14
kidneys
    curried lamb's kidneys 53
kingfish
    Keralan fish curry 97
kodampuli 97
kofte 36
kukupaka 70

Lahore lamb biryani 152–4
lamb
    braised lamb shanks 49–51
    chilli mutton chops 28
    Kashmiri-style rich lamb curry 46
    Lahore lamb biryani 152–4
    lamb browned in its sauce (lamb kosha) 44
    lamb meatball curry 36
    lamb with beetroot 42
    lamb with okra 38
    lamb with potatoes 41
    lamb with whole spices 45
    Pakistani lamb curry 48
    rogan josh shepherd's pie 54–5
lassi
    mango-flavoured yogurt drink (mango lassi) 200
    salty spiced lassi (taaq) 197
lemonade 196
long beans
    potato and long bean curry 122

macher jhol 98
mangoes
    green mango, coconut and cashew nut chutney
        181
    mango-flavoured yogurt drink (mango lassi) 200
    mango pickle 178
    mango salsa 181
    sweet mango curry 112
masala chai 201

masala dosa filling 170
matar paneer 123
matar pullao 144
matthias 17
meatballs
    lamb meatball curry 36
    minty beef meatballs 62–3
meetha pullao 158
methi chicken 79
minty beef meatballs 62–3
mung beans, sprouted salad 16
mustard leaves
    ground greens in the Punjabi style 110
mutton: chilli mutton chops 28

Nagore chicken curry 83
Nepalese potato salad with a sesame dressing 176
nihari 49–51
nimbu pani 196
noodles
    split pea and tomato sauce with noodles 30–33

okra
    dry okra 115
    lamb with okra 38
onion bhajias 19

padora 164
Pakistani lamb curry 48
pakora, pea and potato sabzi 117
pancakes
    potato filling for Southern savoury pancakes 170
    southern savoury pancakes 168–9
    tangy rice pancakes 162
paratha 165–7
peas
    peas with fresh Indian cheese 123
    rice with peas 144
pitla 135
pork
    Ghurka-style pork curry with choi sum 56–8
    Goan pork vindaloo with potatoes 60

potatoes
  cauliflower with potatoes 108
  flatbreads stuffed with potatoes 165–7
  lamb with potatoes 41
  Nepalese potato salad with a sesame dressing 176
  pakora, pea and potato sabzi 117
  potato and long bean curry 122
  potato and spinach curry 120
  potato filling for Southern savoury pancakes 170
  potatoes with fresh fenugreek 118
  roasted masala potatoes 121
prawns
  Goan prawn curry 86
  hot Punjabi king prawn curry 88
  prawn curry with spinach 90
  prawn salad (prawn bharta) 175
pudinay vale kofte 62–3
Punjabi king prawn curry, hot 88

raitas
  beetroot raita 193
  cucumber, onion and mint raita 193
red lentil and chana dal 138
rice
  cashew nut and curry leaf rice 146
  coconut rice 143
  plain yellow rice 142
  rice and mung dal 149
  rice cooked with chicken in an aromatic chicken
      broth 150
  rice with peas 144
  rice with toor dal and vegetables 148–9
  sweet yellow rice 158
rogan josh shepherd's pie 54–5

sabudana usal 23
sabudana vadas 20
salads
  Himalayan salad 174
  Nepalese potato salad with a sesame dressing 176
  prawn salad 175
  sprouted mung bean salad 16
samosas, Gujarati vegetable 25
sarson ka saag 110

seasonings 218
semolina halva 207
sheera 207
sookhi bhindi 115
southern savoury pancakes 168–9
  potato filling for southern savoury pancakes 170
spices, roasting 219
spinach
  ground greens in the Punjabi style 110
  potato and spinach curry 120
split pea and tomato sauce with noodles 30–3
sprouted mung bean salad 16
sukuma wiki 116

taaq 197
tamarind chutney 192
tangy, spicy fruit salad 202
tapioca pearl and sweet potato fry 23
tapioca pearl fritters 20
tarka 219
tikka masala
  Madhur's chicken tikka masala 76–8
tomatoes
  split pea and tomato sauce with noodles 30–3
  tomato chutney 188

vadas 20, 21
vegetable samosas, Gujarati 25
vengan na raviaya 106

yakhni pullao 150
yogurt
  beetroot raita 193
  cucumber, onion and mint raita 193
  mango-flavoured yogurt drink 200
  salty spiced lassi 197
  sweet yogurt 'custard' with cardamom 206
  yogurt sauce with broad beans 136

Acknowledgements

I would like to thank the following, without whose help this book would not have been possible:

Aileen Fernandes, Amit Gupta, Anita Kara, Balwinder Kaur at Punjab'n de Rasoi, Bashan Rafique, Bimal Parmar at Gatundu's, Chennai Sangeetha Restaurant, Claire Fisher at Ganapati, Dharmesh Lakhani at Bobby's, Gurbax Kaur, Ismet Ahmed, Jagdish Kaur at Punjab'n de Rasoi, Kalwant Sahota, Kesang Lama, Lalita and Urvesh at Gujarati Rasoi, Lutfun Hussain, Mahesh Chandra Joshi at Mister Singh's India, Mallika Basu, Meinir Jones-Lewis, Mohammed Azeem at Lahore Kebab House, Mrs Sarla Gupta at Chaat House, Mumtaz Khan at Mumtaz, Naina Parmar, Parul Patel, Pemba Lama, Rajbiar Aulakh, Ranjan Davda, Rohit Chugh at Roti Chai, Rubina Haider, Saleem Zahid, Sarita Udaniya, Sarojini Gulhane, Saumya Singh, Shafiq Rahman, Shayona Restaurant, Sheela Junankar, Sri Guru Singh Sabha Gurdwara in Southall, Sumayya Jamil, Suniya Quoreshi, Surinder Wariabharaj, Tahmima Anam, Vivek Singh at Cinnamon Club, Yesmien Bagh Ali, Zahda Saeed.

I would especially like to thank Nikita Gulhane who worked heroically, night and day, to get all the recipes collected and tested in a very short amount of time.

I would also like to thank Deborah, my agent, for her continued support and optimism, and Lucy Bannell for being the stalwart, patient, and encouraging editor that she is.

And I must thank my grandson, Robi Jaffrey, who worked so hard researching all the material for the introduction and who helped me organise the recipes, chapters and, indeed, the whole book.

The Publisher would like to give special thanks to Nikita Gulhane for all his help and tireless work collecting and developing the recipes (www.spicemonkey.co.uk).

The Publisher would like to thank everyone at Cactus and Good Food Channel for their help in putting this book together, especially Amanda Ross, Dunk Barnes and Nicola Rowley.

Bangladeshi Allotment, www.spitalfieldscityfarm.org; Bimal Parmar at Gatundu's, www.gatundus.co.uk; Bobby's Restaurant, www.eatatbobbys.com; Chennai Sangeetha, www.chennaisangeetha.co.uk; Cinnamon Kitchen, www.cinnamon-kitchen.com; Ganapati, www.ganapatirestaurant.com; Gujarati Rasoi, www.gujaratirasoi.com; Lahore Kebab House, www.lahore-kebabhouse.com; Mallika Basu, www.quickindiancooking.com; Mister Singh's India, www.mistersinghsindia.com; Mumtaz, www.mumtaz.co.uk; Punjab'n de Rasoi, www.edinburghcommunitycafes.org.uk/punjab-n-de-rasoi; Roti Chai, www.rotichai.com; Shayona, www.shayonarestaurants.com; Sri Guru Singh Sabha, www.sgsss.org; Tahmima Anam, www.tahmima.com; Yesmien Bagh Ali, www.amaali.co.uk; Young London Goan Society, www.ylgs.org.uk

Statement from Sikh Sanjog: "For the past 20 years, Sikh Sanjog has challenged the oppression of women, and the creation of the Social Enterprise Community Café has benefited the whole community."